and God bless.

*Suzanne M.
Wilbanks*

Sand
In
Your Heart

Fourth Printing

Suzanne M. Wilbanks

Sand In Your Heart

Suzanne M. Wilbanks

Copyright © 2000
All Rights Reserved

The author has tried to share with the reader the special charm of the Apalachicola area. Many of the town's true landmarks have been incorporated into the story and, with permission, several places and events have been the inspiration for certain parts of the plot. However, this is a work of fiction, and all characters, businesses, dialogues and incidents, while they may bear resemblance to some in the area, are strictly fictional and are not to be construed as real.

PUBLISHED BY:
BRENTWOOD ACADEMIC PRESS
4000 BEALLWOOD AVENUE
COLUMBUS, GEORGIA 31904

Dedication

This book is lovingly dedicated to my parents,
Pleasant Strickland Mitchell
(1921-1991)
and Harry H. Mitchell.

Acknowledgments

I wish to thank the following people for their literary and clerical help: Geri Craig, Anne Little, Barbara Wilbur and Virginia Strickland. Also Bobbie Ames for her publishing suggestions, the special people in Gulf Shores and Orange Beach, Alabama for showing me how wonderful life at the beach can be, and the lovely citizens of Apalachicola for their suggestions and support, especially the late Margaret Harmony Livings Key whose words inspired the title of this book.

In addition, a huge thanks goes to each of my family members for their patience, love, encouragement, and support: Harry Mitchell, my father, Jeannie Mitchell, my sister, Chip and Stan, my brothers and their respective wives, Kim and Lodie, my niece Amber Mitchell, my son Penton Wilbanks, my daughter Paige Wilbanks Lay, my son-in-law, Jim Lay, my precious granddaughter, Hannah Ruth Lay and, finally, my husband, Pat Wilbanks, who gave his support, as well as his office, to this project. As Libbie would say, "I love you all soooo good!"

Prologue

Friday, December 1

Santa Claus grabbed the thick anchor rope which was coiled in a pile at the front of the old sailboat and struggled to regain his balance. His pillow-padded stomach shook like the legendary bowl full of jelly, as the bow of the boat dipped and rose with the waves, and his eyes were definitely twinkling, but not because he was jolly tonight. In fact, the burning moisture behind his lids felt strangely like tears.

"*Nah, I haven't become that sentimental,*" he thought. "*It's probably the salt spray from the bay blowing in my face.*" In fact, his elastic-held, poly-fiber beard was starting to feel a little sticky - saggy too.

The November evening was unusually cool for Florida, and the clear, dark sky was splattered with thousands of stars. The wind was brisk and the waters choppy, but the vintage Governor Stone, the town's historic 1877 Gulf Coast Schooner, skillfully cut through the waves of Apalachicola Bay as if it were her maiden voyage. Santa, however, who had never been on a sailboat in his life, was having a hard time appreciating the historical value of this adventure and found himself wishing for an old-fashioned sleigh - even a helicopter. He knew that both were out of the question. He re-adjusted his beard and turned his thoughts to the anticipated festivities around the bend ahead.

Each year, the folks in Apalachicola, Florida, a quaint, picturesque fishing village on Apalachicola Bay off of the Gulf of Mexico, officially began their Christmas season on the Friday night following Thanksgiving. In preparation, citizens decorated the downtown, stringing Christmas lights across the streets, covering the streetlamp posts with Santa faces, and putting candles in the storefront windows. Vendors set up hot dog, cotton candy, and hot chocolate stands, small circus rides were set up in a vacant lot near the docks, and Christmas music was heard on every street corner. Shortly after dark, thousands of tiny lights would magically glow on the town's giant Christmas tree, signaling the official start of the gala, but only after the traditional sighting of Santa as he sailed up the Apalachicola River on the Governor Stone.

"What's the matter, fatso? You leave your sea legs at home?" his friend, Cap'n Jimbo, called from the back of the boat as he expertly maneuvered the stately old lady around a shallow bar and into the channel. "It's cold as a well-digger's shovel out here!" Jimbo continued. "Why don't you come on back and have some of Shelley's hot chocolate? We won't dock this little lady for a few more minutes yet."

The thought of hot chocolate on his already unsettled stomach had little appeal to Santa who had foolishly not eaten before he left home. Besides, he was in more of a reflective than talkative mood tonight and preferred to stay up front for the rest of the ride. After all, this was his special debut, and he wanted to savor the moment.

"Thanks man," he called back, careful not to let go of the rope as he turned. "I think I'll just stay around up here. Hey, somebody's got to keep watch to make sure that you don't run into anything," he added jokingly.

Just ahead, Santa could already hear the unmistakable twang of the high school brass ensemble drifting across the water. They were playing a somewhat recognizable version of *Joy to the World*. He chuckled as he remembered Mrs. Emmaline Harris putting in her special request for some religious music this year at the festivities. "Let's not forget," she reminded the committee; "Jesus is the reason for the season, you know." However, no one, not even Mrs. Harris, would object when the little band broke into *Here Comes Santa Claus*.

He fondly thought of his many friends other than Mrs. Harris who were awaiting his arrival. He could expect to see Old Mr. Jones and Mr. Hankins, along with other old-timers, patriarchs of the town who whittled the mornings away in front of the hardware store and discussed politics with a vengeance. They had told him they would be setting up a table down by the docks to sell their carvings - most of them wooden Christmas ornaments. And Mrs. Harris and her niece, Libbie, were planning to sell hot herbal tea near the Christmas tree, where Sam Penton, Owner and Managing Editor of *The Village Voice* would be set up to take pictures of the children in Santa's lap. He smiled with pride when he remembered that little Jody Parramore had made his mother take him to the docks right after school so he could be first in line for a picture.

The youth choir from Reverend Matt's church would be singing Christmas Carols, and Jimmy Johns and his friend, Rex, would be riding around town on their decorated bikes passing out certificates for a free visit to the exercise room at the new Rehabilitation Facility.

Without warning, the old schooner groaned and banked to the left. "Lean to the right, Fatso," Jimbo called from the rear. "We're heading around the bend."

Just ahead, the festive lights of the village lit up the shoreline, their reflection twinkling in the waters of the river. Crowds were lined along the docks clapping and yelling, and Santa found himself overwhelmed with emotion. Once again he felt his eyes misting, and he experienced an unfamiliar tug at his heart...

Only last week, Mrs. Wilburn, his neighbor, had told him, "Son, when people move to Florida, they get sand in their shoes. But when they move to Apalachicola, the sand gets into their bloodstream, and then into their heart."

"*Yeah,*" he thought. *"I wonder if it starts in the eyes."*

FLORIDA

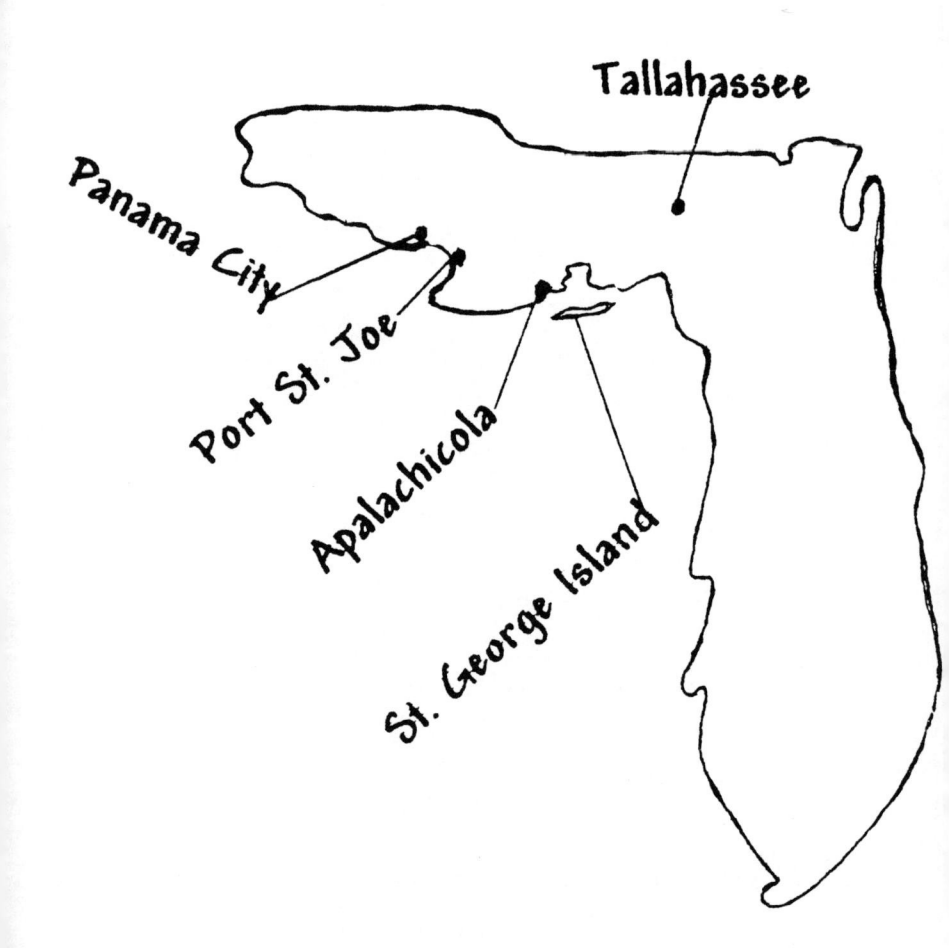

Chapter 1

*To save energy, don't go out lookin' for trouble;
chances are it'll find you soon enough!*

Forest Gump

Seven months earlier
Friday, May 25

Spring was dragging its feet this year, a fact which had neither dismayed nor overly concerned the locals in the peaceful, little historic fishing village of Apalachicola, Florida....that is, until the tornado.

The unsuspecting, sleepy citizens had awakened to an early-morning, massive seasonal thunderstorm that rumbled in off of the Gulf of Mexico around daybreak. It relentlessly attacked the village, spawning a fierce tornado that roared through several neighborhoods, toyed with the roofs and awnings of downtown buildings, and finally, bounced along the bay devouring several boats and an old dock before swirling back into the clouds, its circular winds digesting the remnants of its escapade.

In its wake, the startled townspeople had ventured out into an amazingly fresh, clear morning in which the sun was shining and the birds singing as if nothing of significance had happened. Out along Highway 98 by the bay, folks were surveying their damage with a rather curious fascination.

"I've been telling y'all we better pay attention to that El Niño thing," a crusty old fisherman remarked to a group of curious onlookers. "Now see here, it's done spit a tornado at us, and folks, you can mark my words, there's gonna be more." Pointing to his right, he continued, "Yep, that thing must of come in over them trees yonder by Smitty's Bait Shop. See where it bounced cross th' yard an' flattened that old eighteen wheeler trailer? Oh well, good riddance, I say. I reckon Ol' Smitty ain't been in that thing for years. Its just been sitting there like an old eye sore, with kudzu vines growin' all over it."

The verbose charter boat captain from days gone by stuck his thumbs in his empty belt loops and hiked up his britches an inch or two, only to have them fall back down when he leaned over to spit out a stream of tobacco juice. Wiping the dribble off of his gnarly beard with the back of his leathery hand, he continued.

"Reckon y'all heard what washed up in the inlet next to that ol' trailer, didn't you?" He flashed a snaggle-toothed grin at the curious, gathering crowd.

"Yep,...Smitty and the boys, they found a body over yonder. It looks like the ol' boy was shot before somebody threw him in that little piece of water; musta had bricks or somethin' in his clothes to weigh him down. Reckon that storm stirred them waters up somethin' fierce, cause that sucker washed up on shore with his britches tore clean off him!"

Cautiously watching from a short distance, a lone figure in sagging jeans and a dirty, ripped T-shirt walked slowly along the water's edge, his bare feet crunching uncomfortably on the ragged, discarded oyster shells from the area's fish houses. His tangled, black, shoulder length hair blew across his face, covering his eyes enough to allow him to observe the nearby activity without being obvious.

"It's a good thing I was out on the island last night, or I would have been flattened in that ol' trailer," he thought.

His stomach growled, and his head throbbed, as he watched several curious people around the trailer picking through what was left of his belongings. Thank goodness there weren't many personal items in his little temporary, make-shift home; a few toiletries, his one pair of shoes, and a shirt or two shouldn't arouse too much suspicion. His main concern was checking on the important stuff he had stashed in the old propane tank out behind the trailer. He'd just have to be patient a little longer; maybe they would go away soon.

Blast! What were the stinking cops coming for? They were probably just making routine stops, but he didn't like it. *"Maybe it's time I was moving on, anyway,"* he surmised with a shrug. *"A person can't get too relaxed in a little place like this."*

Tucking in his shirt, a futile effort for someone with no waist, and running his fingers through his hair, he made a reckless attempt to appear somewhat presentable as he turned and headed in the opposite direction toward the 24-Hour Stop and Shop. He figured he better pay for the sugar doughnuts and orange juice today, things that he usually pocketed for free... no need to push his luck.

The middle-aged lady at the cash register was in such heavy conversation with her customer, that she didn't even notice him come in, let alone notice that he was barefooted.

The sign on the door plainly stated,
"NO SHOES, NO SHIRT - NO SERVICE!"

The younger girl at the counter was in a talkative mood, as she paid for her cigarettes and Coke. "Hey Mavis, did I tell you that me and the girls at Minute Maids got us a new house-cleaning job out on St. George

Island?" she asked. "It's that big house down on West End. I'm fixin' to pick up Paula, and we're going out there this morning. Girl, I'm gonna earn me some good spending money for this evening. By the way, Mavis, is your husband gonna let you go with us girls tonight?"

"Honey, my husband don't even believe there is such a thing as them male dancers," Mavis answered. "He says no decent, self-respectin' man would parade around doing that for a living, and if there was any such guys, it's for sure they wouldn't be comin' to Apalachicola, Florida. Anyways, I told him, 'Ralph, they are too coming, to the legion house in Carrabelle, and the girls want me to go with them.' Now, if he don't want to believe it, that's his problem, ain't it?

"Besides, did I say anything when him and his buddies went to that National Monster Truck Convention last month and spent the night over in Jacksonville?" Mavis winked at her friend and stuck another piece of gum in her mouth. "No ma'am, I sure didn't. So, what time are you girls gonna pick me up?"

"Stupid broads!" he thought. *"I wish they'd hurry up. They're all alike. Those two would probably be...."*

Then he saw it....

"No! It couldn't be."

There she was, smiling at him from the front page of *The Village Voice*. His heart started racing and he noticed that his hands were shaking when he finally reached the counter to pay for his food and newspaper.

"Man, what's wrong with me?" he thought. *"That tornado musta really messed with my nerves; it's probably those stupid cob-webs in my brain again. That last hit I bought from Scotty must have been full of crud. Anyway, why would she be living here, of all places? But, what if it's really her? Yeah, this might be just what I've been looking for. Sure, wasn't she always telling me that junk about God loving me, and she did too? Well, we'll just see about that. It's time my luck changed anyway, and she might be just the person to help make it happen. Maybe this little place ain't so bad after all."*

Mavis yelled at his back as he walked out of the door. "Hey buddy, don't be comin' in here no more without ya shoes on."

"The name's not 'buddy,' ma'am," he mumbled under his breath, "and if I owned some shoes, lady, I'd be wearing them."

Outside, he crammed the doughnuts in his mouth and threw the wrapper in a trash can in front of the store. Leaning against the side of the building, he casually checked out the parking lot. When he was satisfied that no one was watching, he strolled over to the Minute Maid van and jiggled the back door handle. It easily pulled open, and he crawled in, surveying the clutter of cleaning supplies piled in the back; vacuum cleaners, buckets, brooms, mops, pieces of stained rags, and tote bags full of various bottles and spray cans. An old stained blanket was wadded up in the far back corner. Quickly making his way through the mess, he curled up under the musty cover in the back, leaving a small opening for breath.

The air inside the closed-up van was stifling with an irritating smell of disinfectant which burned his nose, threatening to make him sneeze. For a fleeting moment he considered changing his mind, but the decision was made for him when the driver's door opened and a large purse was thrown into the back, missing his head by inches.

Chapter 2

Consider the girdle; its support is very much like that of family and friends - strong and reliable.
                                              Paige W. Lay

Several miles away in the lovely, historic Harbor Heights neighborhood, a different kind of clean-up effort was taking place. Libbie Whitestone, recent widow of the town's most adored pediatrician, Dr. Robert Whitestone, was preparing her home for a dinner party, unaware of the severity of the tornado destruction just blocks away. Her neighborhood had been graciously spared, and the most damage that she had seen was her overturned garbage can. She and her aunt, Emmaline Harris, had spent the morning ironing cotton napkins, polishing the silverware, and dusting, among other things.

"WHO DIED now?" Aunt Emma called out, adjusting her hearing aid as she straightened slightly in her creaky wooden rocker. Although often found there, she seldom rocked in the chair because she had decided that it affected her equilibrium, which, in turn, brought on fits of dizziness, possible nausea and, of course, justifiable disorientation. However, she had insisted on moving her garage-sale bargain chair into Libbie's tastefully decorated den, because Libbie's upholstered furniture was too soft - bad for her back. Also, she was quick to point out, upholstery fabrics retained dust and odors which might induce sneezing, a sure way to throw her back out.

"NO one died, Aunt Emma," her niece called back from across the room. "I said, I'm trying to DECIDE HOW to arrange this room for Couple's Supper Club tonight, and I need to bring in extra chairs so that we can all eat together." Libbie Whitestone once again prayed for the patience that so often seemed to elude her these days.

The older lady balanced precariously on the edge of her rocker as she exclaimed, "Oh double darn. I forgot to get my blue Sunday dress from the cleaners, and my hair's a mess. I needed a touch-up this week, and wouldn't you know that lazy Velma would decide to close for repairs. Well, I say she better be repairing her marriage instead of running around at night going to those meetings.

"Now," she continued, "what were you saying Dearie?"

"It's not important, Emmy. Why don't you decide where to put the hors'doeuvres while I bring in some more chairs."

Emmaline Harris, Libbie's 78-year-old aunt and her mother's only living sibling, had come to Apalachicola in the autumn of '95 to be of help after Libbie's husband, Robert, had been killed. Retired after 40 years of teaching high school English in Panama City, Florida, Emmaline had been a vibrant, feisty, take-charge person, even in her advancing years. Now, over a year later, she was a very permanent resident in the Whitestone house and one whose eccentric but loving presence would be sorely missed should she move on. The latter was doubtful, as she had become as dependent on Libbie and the twins as they were on her.

Libbie's mind wandered fondly back to that autumn morning when Aunt Emma had arrived on her doorstep with her small, green Samsonite suitcase, vintage 1950, in her hands, her umbrella hanging over her right arm and her black pillbox hat threatening to fall off of her fuzzy gray head. She had swept through the front door, given her niece a hasty but loving kiss on the cheek and set about taking care of the matters at hand. "Nothing more than your mother would have done, God rest her soul," Aunt Emma had claimed as she had unpacked and settled in. "Now you just leave the household matters to me so that you can spend more time with your attorney and that nice Sheriff Coggins. The sooner you can sort through the details, the better."

Aunt Emma's steady, loving presence had been the soothing balm so needed by Libbie and the twins, Trish and Travis, during the pain-filled months of doubt and speculation following Rob's accident. To this day no acceptable explanation had been found for the fact that the brake lines on his mangled truck appeared to have been cut, and the case was still in the active file. However, Libbie had seen few signs of any current investigative activity, something which bothered her greatly. She made a mental note to call Bernie Coggins this week.

Although Libbie's strong church background and steadfast faith had provided a mystifying strength throughout her ordeal, she still struggled daily with an overwhelming need for answers and closure. Her feelings of helplessness often reverted to loneliness, an emotion that was very much magnified each time she attended Couples Supper Club. Tonight would be the first time that the group had met in her home since Rob's death.

The insistent ring of the doorbell brought her thoughts back to the matters at hand, specifically the stack of folding chairs standing in the corner. "Should I put those out in the den or bring in my dining room chairs?" she remarked, more to herself than to Aunt Emma who, she noticed, was now dozing peacefully in her rocker with Repeat, the old gray, furry cat, nestled in her lap. Libbie headed toward the front door and was rewarded with the smiling face of one of her favorite people.

"Afternoon Miz Libbie. Here's your paper, and look-a-here. They already got pictures of the tornado mess on the front page. Them newspaper reporters is fast ain't they?" Jimmy Johns said. "Oh, and here's a package fer Miz Emma. Another one of them things she orders from the catalogues, I reckon."

"Oh dear, I suppose you're right, Jimmy. I wonder what it is? You know, I try to hide the catalogues as soon as you bring them, but she seems to have radar where those things are concerned," Libbie laughed. "Do you remember the last thing she ordered? It was that door knob alarm, guaranteed to send out a siren each time anyone opened the door. As you know she doesn't hear well, and likes to know when someone comes in. The funny thing was that most of the time she couldn't hear the alarm when it sounded, so she decided that it didn't work and put it in the church rummage sale."

"Yes um, I remember that, all right," Jimmy Johns answered with a shy grin.

Libbie's heart went out to the scrawny, sandy-haired young man. He had been the town's unofficial adopted son for as long as she could remember, living all of his thirty-odd years on the outskirts of town with his invalid mother in a small house trailer. Jimmie had never completed school; his teachers had said that he was just too slow to learn. He was a hard worker, however, holding down two jobs. During the day he did maintenance and yard work at the historic First United Methodist Church, and on his way home each afternoon, he delivered the afternoon *Democrat* to the houses along Libbie's route. Several of Libbie's neighbors, including Libbie herself, also enjoyed Jimmy's extra gesture of bringing the mail from their boxes out by the street, a practice for which they periodically showed their appreciation with everything from food to money.

Some of the townspeople affectionately called Jimmy "Preacher Man," as he loved to ride around town on his bicycle, wearing a different baseball cap each day (gifts from his many friends) and quoting Bible verses or singing church hymns. However, Aunt Emma would have no part of this nickname stuff, as she said that boy's mother had named him Jimmy for a reason, and it wasn't up to her to change it! Libbie had continued to call him Jimmy, more out of habit than out of an effort to appease Emma.

Libbie returned Jimmy's contagious smile and said, "Thank you so much, Jimmy. Is that all for me today?"

"Yes ma'am, unless you wanna hear the new Bible verse I learned this week at the men's Prayer Breakfast."

"Oh yes, of course, Jimmy. You know how much I love to hear your verses and songs."

Jimmy beamed as he looked up and recited from Psalms, almost to perfection: "Turn to me and be gracious to me, for I is — no, I *am* lonely and afflicted."

Libbie smiled as she silently completed the verses which had been a constant prayer of hers over the last year and a half: "The troubles of my heart are enlarged: Bring me out of my distresses."

Whoever said that Jimmy couldn't learn?

"Oh Jimmy, I think you must be one of God's special messengers today. That verse was just what I needed to hear this afternoon. Thank you so much, my friend."

Jimmy hummed all the way down the long sidewalk, turning back to wave several times. As he wheeled off on his bicycle, he expertly veered around the delivery boy from Bouquets by the Bay.

The card on the box of flowers was for Ms. Libbie Whitestone and simply read,

Looking forward to this evening.
Matt

* * *

Libbie felt foolishly like a school girl as she arranged the lovely yellow roses in her mother's cut glass vase. They were a beautiful complement to the soft peaches and aquas in her den. Had Matt remembered the colors in her home from that one visit? Surely not...

She had redecorated her home the previous fall after she and Shelley had gone to Atlanta to shop and have their colors done. Most of their friends had been color-analyzed years ago, and she was probably one of the last ones in town to indulge herself. Nevertheless, the timing could not have been more perfect for her, as it had been just the lift she needed after a year of grief and mourning.

She had been diagnosed as having a Spring palette because of her strawberry blonde hair, blue-green eyes, and skin with pink undertones. Her accompanying "portfolio" suggested that she surround herself with the clear, bright (sometimes soft) colors of spring, those with yellow and orange tones, avoiding colors that were heavy and dark, with pink, black or gray tones. In addition, the profile of a Spring suggested that she might be soft, delicate, easy-going and gentle.

The analyzation had been amazingly helpful and somewhat correct, except for the fact that Libbie was anything but easy-going! In fact, these days she seemed to be almost wired, her mind constantly racing and her body seeming to have more and more trouble keeping up with it. Her delicate frame now carried an unwanted extra eight pounds that just wouldn't seem to go away.

That new OB/GYN in town had suggested that she might be showing signs of early menopause but, at 42, Libbie wasn't ready to hear such foolishness. Why, all she needed to do was start playing tennis again and maybe join that new exercise class at the church. Besides, Neal Roper, Rob's former partner, had said that her nerves could play all kind of tricks on her mind and body, and even though he was a children's doctor, she trusted his judgment far more than that of some new young doctor fresh out of medical school.

"Libbie, why do you suppose that butterflies are called butterflies?" Aunt Emma called, awakening from her short nap and bringing Libbie's thoughts, once again, back to the present. "I mean, what do they have to do with butter? Oh, I know that some of them are yellow," she continued, "but surely that has nothing to do with it...Now if I was still teaching, I would give that as an extra credit assignment.

"By the way, where did you get those beautiful yellow roses? Seeing them made me think of butterflies, you know."

"Yes, Aunt Emma, I can see how they might," Libbie patronized. "And I have no idea about the origin of the word butterfly. Why don't you ask the twins now that they're home from college for the summer. Give them something constructive to think about.

"The flowers are from the new minister at Riverside Congregational," she added. "His name's Matthew Douglas, and I met him last weekend at Jimbo and Shelley Hopkins' barbecue. Several of our friends invited him to join us for supper club tonight. He is staying at Shelley and Jimbo's Hopkins' House Inn until his house is finished on the island."

Emmaline Harris sat up straighter than usual and smiled. "There's a new Reverend in town? And he's sending you flowers?" she asked. "Well, Hallelujah, Missy. I'm certainly glad to see you interested in someone other than that fast-talking lawyer from the city. Remember I have pretty good instincts about these things," Emmaline reminded her. "Did you say the Reverend's bringing the barbecue? You know you shouldn't ask a guest to bring something the very first visit, especially if you want to see more of him."

"No, Aunt Emma; he's not bringing anything," Libbie responded, louder now that she realized Emmaline must not have her hearing aid turned completely on. "I said I met him at a barbecue....and I'm certainly not interested in any man as more than a friend, so tell your instincts to relax for a while. Besides, other than Travis, old Pete is as much male as either of us needs around here."

Hearing his name, Pete, the lovable but mischievous cocker ambled over to the sofa and laid his floppy head on Libbie's lap.

"Come on, boy. Let's go over and show Repeat and Aunt Emma how much we love them," she whispered.

The two of them started across the room, but not quietly enough to keep from arousing Repeat, who wanted nothing to do with the bothersome cocker today. The cat sprang from the chair as they approached and hissed a warning, just in case Pete was in a playful mood. Libbie bent down and affectionately kissed her aunt on the forehead, as she carefully adjusted the hearing aids behind Emmaline's glasses.

"Here's the phone, Emmy," Libbie said, using her affectionate nickname for Emmaline. "Would you answer it while I'm gone? I need to run to Sylvia's Diner at the Docks to pick up my meat for tonight.

"By the way, the twins are planning some kind of cookout on St. George Island tonight. They may already be out there, but if one of them comes home, even for a minute, would you tell them to please bring the dining room chairs in and put them over in front of the bookshelves? Thanks, Emmy....and you know, I still love you soooo good!" she said, repeating their well-worn phrase from Libbie's childhood.

Chapter 3

I've had a wonderful evening - but this wasn't it!
Groucho Marx

The first star of the evening twinkled far out over the horizon where the peaceful ocean waters surrounding St. George Island, five miles out in the Gulf of Mexico, met the evening sky. A low, orange moon slowly rose in the East, illuminating phosphorescent sparkles dancing on the tops of gentle, rolling waves. How amazing that the evening could be so lovely, when only this morning a violent storm, spawning the frightful tornado, had moved across the area leaving such devastation in its wake!

Libbie's daughter, Trish Whitestone, shivered slightly in the late May breeze as she moved the blanket a little closer to the bonfire. She marveled at the beauty of God's universe, now so peacefully revealing itself as if to say, "Here I am, Trish, glowing tonight just for you. Welcome home."

Although the picturesque island was not actually home, throughout the years the area locals had grown accustomed to claiming it as their own, a habit that would not die quickly despite the hoards of new property owners moving in from around the country everyday. Controversy aside, all parties involved claimed that the long, narrow island had the most beautiful, unspoiled, white, sandy beaches in the world. For Trish, the beach had never seemed lovelier than at this moment.

"Come on, Sassy. Don't hog the blanket. You're wrapped up like a squaw over there, and you didn't even go swimming; I'm the one standing here shivering in my wet bathing suit."

Trish smiled at Wes' familiar use of her nickname. "Poor baby," she teased. "Why don't you put your shirt on? You know, I'm surprised that they even let wimps like you play linebacker at Florida State." She leaned back and raised her hands to her eyes as if focusing a camera on the big two-hundred pound athlete. "How about this scoop, folks; 'Wes Culpepper, big Senior on campus, afraid of a little chill.' If the word gets out, Baby Face, your reputation is doomed. It's probably a good thing I go to school in another state so I can talk about you without completely ruining your image."

Her taunting had the predicted effect; Wes easily swooped her up in his arms and headed for the water. "Hey babe, you've gotten a little too sassy this last semester," he said. "I'm thinking you need a little reality check, maybe a swim to clear your pretty head."

"OK, OK....sorry big guy. Come on; put me down ....please, Trish pleaded. "I really don't want to get wet tonight."

Hand in hand the couple headed back towards the bonfire. They had each arrived home for the summer the past week, and tonight was the first time that they had been alone...or almost alone.

Travis, Trish's twin brother and Wes's buddy from high school, had intruded on their little beach outing at the last minute when he had asked the new girl in town, Rachel Morgan, for a date.

"Hey, why don't we join you guys," Travis had suggested, "since I really don't know this Rachel girl. I just met her yesterday at Caro's coffee shop and took a chance on asking her out for tonight. Man, I couldn't believe it when she said 'yes.' I mean, she's drop-dead gorgeous.

"When I introduced myself," he continued, "she asked me if my mom was Libbie Whitestone. You know this is a small place and all, but listen to this...she said that her parents are going to Mom's tonight as visitors to her supper club.

"Anyway, her family has bought that huge house on the island that used to belong to the governor. I was thinking that maybe the four of us could build a bonfire down on the beach there in front of her place where nobody would probably even notice, since her parents are going to be up in town and the house is so far down on the end of the island."

The couples had indeed found the perfect secluded area and snuggled in for a relaxed evening by the fire, a welcome change from the hectic exam week that each had just completed. And finally, for the first time all evening, Trish and Wes found themselves alone. Putting his football jersey on, as Trish had suggested, Wes dropped down on the blanket next to her and pushed his wet hair out of his face.

"Hey, where are Travis and Rachel?" he asked.

"Actually, I thought that Travis was with you," replied Trish. "He got up right after you left to find firewood and said he would go help you. About that same time, Rachel thought that she heard her dog whining and ran up to the house to check on him."

"Yeah, well I never saw him, so I'm assuming that the two of them are together somewhere. Boy, that Travis is smooth, isn't he?"

"I don't know, Wes. Maybe we ought to go check on them. They've been gone for quite a while now."

"Aw, Trish, come on, relax. Do you really think your brother wants a chaperone on his first date with a Miss Miami calendar girl? And anyway, I'm glad to finally have you all to myself for a while."

Anticipating a snide comment from Trish on his observation of Rachel, Wes squeezed her in a giant bear hug, reaching up to pinch her nose. During the past few years that they had been dating, this had become his affectionate way of saying "Shut up Trish."

Trish swatted his hand away, grinning at the gentle giant with the pudgy, little boy cheeks. She found herself, once again, irresistibly drawn to his refreshing candor and tenderness. As she snuggled into the comfortable security of his arms, she reflected on how important their relationship had become to her.

"Hey, Baby Face," she whispered. "I've missed you."

"Yeah? Well I've missed you more," Wes replied in a husky voice.

* * *

A shrill scream pierced through the night air, sending yet another chill through Trish.

"Wes, that sounded like Rachel," she whispered.

"Nah, that came from the sand dunes behind us. You said that she headed down the beach to her house. Besides, we hardly know her well enough to recognize her scream."

"Maybe not, but her house is kind of up behind us to the right a little way. And whoever it was, they were nearby and they were certainly upset."

"I know, I know," Wes said quietly, putting his finger to his lips. "Be quiet, and stay right here while I go check."

Trish grabbed his shirt. "No way," she whispered. "I'm going with you."

The full moon provided plenty of search light as they entered the scrub brush and sand dunes. At the same time, they felt completely vulnerable and exposed, with few places to hide if they came upon an uncomfortable situation.

They moved quietly and slowly over the very dunes on which Trish and Travis had played as children, and Trish experienced an overwhelming sense of deja vu, attributing it to long-ago memories of hide and seek. She had the uncanny urge to giggle, a not uncommon reaction when she was nervous.

Suddenly Wes stopped and knelt behind a sand dune, pulling Trish down beside him.

"I think I see something over by that bush. This time I'm going to check it out alone, Trish, and I mean that I want you to stay right here," he whispered. "If you see someone coming, you run like crazy to the Foster house down the beach and call for help."

"But Wes, what if —."

"Hey, Sassy, don't worry," he said for the second time that night. "It's probably nothing but a beach mouse."

Watching him disappear into the shadows, Trish unconsciously held her breath, as if the sound of her breathing might alert the unknown and reveal her presence - to whom, or what? Seconds seemed like hours before Wes ran out into the clearing, motioning for her to come quickly. She slid down the dune behind which she had hidden, brushed the sand off of her hands, and ran to his side, praying all the way.

Chapter 4

Courage is resistance to fear, mastery of fear, not absence of fear.

Mark Twain

Trish heard the low moan just seconds before she saw the body, partially obscured by the bushes and shadows. She immediately recognized Rachel's long, tan legs, the very ones that she had envied earlier in the evening. A fleeting sense of remorse attacked her momentarily, quickly replaced by concern for the girl's condition.

"Wes, is she OK? she whispered. "What happened to her? Can she talk?"

"Shh, Trish. She seems to be drifting in and out of consciousness, and she's mumbling something; I think it's Travis' name. You're the pre-med student — why don't you come see about her while I look around for a minute."

"No, Wes," she hissed. "You're not going off and leave me again. Let's just see if we can move her and take her to her house. Besides, Travis must be in trouble too, and we've got to get help."

Trish gently checked for fractures as quickly as possible, hindered by the shadows and the girl's restlessness. "Look, here's a huge bump on the back of her head, but I don't see any bleeding. Nothing seems to be broken. Why don't you pick her up and let's just get out of here."

"Yeah, you're probably right," Wes whispered. "I'll get Rachel while you get her shoe over there."

"Okay.... and Wes, this time follow me towards those trees. I know this area like the back of my hand, and there's a shortcut that will lead us right to Rachel's side yard."

The short trip was uneventful until they reached the vacant lot next to the landscaped yard of the huge house. The sandy clearing was still damp and slightly packed from the morning's storm, and two sets of footprints led from the back of the yard to the middle of the open area. Beyond that point, only one set, the larger ones, continued toward the very path that Trish and Wes had just taken.

"Look, Wes," Trish exclaimed, louder than she meant to. "What do you think?"

"Well, Sassy, it looks to me like Rachel was running from someone, and apparently he caught her. Those larger prints are definitely from a man's shoes, and I bet if you put Rachel's shoes in the smaller prints, you'd find that they're hers."

"You're probably right, but let's don't stop to investigate. I'm ready to get to a phone and leave that to someone else."

* * *

"G-get Pep — Traa —." Rachel moaned from the plush sofa in the sun room of her home. Hearing her mumble, Wes sprinted across the room and kneeled by the sofa.

"Hey, Rachel, take it easy. Everything's OK now. You're home, and the paramedics are on the way to check you out. And besides, Trish is a pre-"

"Go s-see about him," She interrupted frantically, as her eyes started to roll back in her head.

"See about who, Rachel? Are you talking about Travis? Come on girl, talk to me," Wes pleaded. "Don't stop now!"

"Hey, Trish," he yelled. "Rachel's mumbling something, but she's not making much sense. What do I do?"

Trish put her hand over the phone receiver and called back, "Try to keep her awake, Wes. She probably has a concussion. I'm talking to Sheriff Coggins, and I'll be there in just a minute"

"Well, you'd better hurry, Sassy, 'cause she's sinking fast."

Trish grabbed a bag that she had filled with ice while talking on the phone and hurried into the sun room.

"Hey, lighten up," she said to Wes who was scowling in Rachel's face while shaking her shoulders. "What are you trying to do? Scare her to death?"

"Whoa, Sassy; I'm doing my best," Wes countered. "This isn't something that I have any training in, you know, so you might want to come help me if we're going to get any information out of her at all. She was trying to tell me something while ago, and I think it was about Travis."

"Oh, Babe; I'm sorry. I'm just scared and frustrated," Trish groaned as she applied the ice bag to the back of Rachel's head. "I don't know what I would do if you weren't here." Speaking a little softer, she said, "And you're right; we've got to find out what she knows, but we need to keep her calm too. Did you see how dilated her pupils are? And her pulse is very weak. I imagine she has a concussion on top of being in shock."

The wail of sirens interrupted their dilemma, promising help and relief. The volunteer paramedics on the island had recently received state recognition for their promptness and efficiency, a fact greatly appreciated by Wes and Trish at the moment.

Wes hurried out on the porch to meet the paramedics and the ambulance, while Trish turned her full attention to the girl on the sofa.

"OK, Hon, now listen. You're going to the hospital so they can take care of the bump on your head. Someone is calling your parents, and I'm sure they'll meet you there. You're going to be just fine," she soothed. "But before you go, I need to know where Travis is. Can you tell me that?"

The girl's eyes filled with tears as she tried to nod her head, mumbling, "With Pepper - in the garage."

* * *

"Stupid jerks! Why did they have to come snooping around just when I was about to hit pay dirt! I thought those bimbo minute maids said nobody would be home out here tonight. I shoulda listened better to their conversation, but hey, who could hear in the back of that rattle-trap under that durn old smelly blanket...

"Yeah, I bet those people had some joints somewhere in that big fancy place... Well, at least I got some shoes and some cash, and a few good-looking pieces of jewelry. The cash ought to hold me until Scotty makes contact. I just wish he would hurry up. I can't get to my stash back in town, with all them cops and people snooping around.

"Man I wonder if I really hurt that blonde broad bad. Nah, I couldn't have hit her that hard. Crud, I hope that other dude didn't get a good look at me!"

The lanky fellow was gasping for breath after running and lugging the pillow case full of stolen goods through the briars, scrub brush and scrawny pines in the back woods near the bay, and his arms and face were scratched and bleeding. He scolded himself for indulging in the greasy fried chicken and baked beans that he had found earlier in the refrigerator at the mansion. The pain in his side was now testimony to his gluttony and was slowing down his escape. However, the nearby sound of barking dogs spurred him on toward the back waters of the island.

"Dang, what if they've got the hounds out after me," he thought frantically. Giving himself a pep talk, he pushed ahead, knowing that the old docks were nearby. *"If I can just get to the raft, maybe I'll be okay. Those stupid dogs can't pick me up in the water. I'll just have to hide out up in that mossy inlet again until they're gone, then I can go back to the old cottage where I was last night. Man, like I've gotta be more careful. I almost messed up big time tonight. Something's gotta give soon.*

Chapter 5

Though nothing can bring back the hour of splendor in the grass, glory in the flower, we will grieve not, rather find strength in what remains behind.

William Wordsworth

Back in town, the rising full moon softly bathed Libbie Whitestone's beautifully manicured lawn with a warm, welcoming glow. Her lovely, white, Victorian two-story home, built in 1891, was one of three houses on Harbor Street listed on the Historic Register. It proudly displayed a grace and dignity so characteristic of older homes, radiant with a charm which seemed to beckon all who passed by to slow down and come relax in one of the wicker rockers on the wide front porch, sip lemonade under the hanging ferns, and make memories while watching the world go by.

The two massive oak trees out front, much older than the house itself, draped their protective limbs over the yard, as if carefully guarding the secrets of their children who, throughout the years, had climbed into their supportive arms. Libbie Borden Whitestone had been one of those children, as had her grandfather Borden.

Tonight the Borden / Whitestone home had a festive air about it, and Libbie felt a special pride as she welcomed her guests. She had actually dreaded this evening, her solo debut without Rob, but the comfortable familiarity of the old home seemed to be casting a magical, tranquil spell on her. *"Maybe, just maybe,"* she thought, *"things will be all right after all."*

Bob and Vickie Callaway, the latter her childhood friend since their three year old dance class, were the first to arrive, bringing as their guests Rachel's parents.

"Hi Lib," Vickie said with a hug. "These are our new friends from the island, Vince and Claire Morgan. You know I told you about them buying Governor Bell's home."

Vickie was one of the more active real estate agents on St. George Island, and although Libbie was proud of her friend's success, she missed the time that they used to spend together.

Libbie graciously extended her hand to each of the Morgans.

"It's nice to meet you, and I'm so glad that you could join us," she said. "I actually feel like I already know you. I've heard quite a bit about you from Vickie, and my son, Travis, hasn't stopped talking about your daughter, Rachel, since he met her yesterday. I believe that they were going somewhere this evening with my daughter and her boyfriend."

Vince Morgan held her hand longer than necessary as he lavished very polished compliments. He had a quick, almost abrasive accent, disturbingly different from the smooth, relaxed speech of north Floridians who tended to sound like and identify more with their neighbors in Georgia and Alabama than their fellow southern Floridians down the state.

"How nice of you to have us, my dear. Your home is quite charming. It's so delightful to find such beauty in the area," he remarked with a raised eyebrow and a slightly rakish grin which would have made Rhett Butler proud.

His wife, Claire, smiled with a strained grin; she simply said "Hello." Trish wondered whether she was shy, irritated with her husband's advances, or just simply aloof, looking down her tan Miami nose at their little society.

Pulling her hand away, Libbie moved towards the living room, Aunt Emma's official territory with the hors' doeuvres.

"Please come in and meet my Aunt Emmaline," she said. "Vickie, why don't you make the introductions while I go to the door. You know Aunt Emma loves to play hostess, and I'm sure she'll take good care of you."

"Oh yes, she'll take care of that Romeo, all right," Libbie thought, smugly. *"He'll meet his match the minute he tries to dazzle her with his practiced charm."* She could barely conceal an amused grin as she headed back to the front door to greet the Reverend Douglas.

"Oh Matt, welcome, and thank you so much for the beautiful roses. They look wonderful on the coffee table, and the color is just perfect."

Matthew Douglas smiled as he took Libbie's extended hand.

"I'm glad you like them, Libbie. Actually, I'm the one who should be thanking you for having me as a guest tonight. I knew that your house would already look great without any help from me, but I know how most women hate to receive candy, so I figured you could use the flowers somewhere."

Libbie warmed quickly to the Reverend's honesty as well as his perception. She wondered how his wife could have possibly failed to appreciate him.

Rumor had it that the former Mrs. Douglas had become severely addicted to drugs - mainly pain-killers, following a series of surgeries. It was said that her faithful husband had taken her to the best clinics in Texas, but she had never seemed to improve for long.

According to Mildred Vickery, who had forever been the unofficial "social chairwoman" at Riverside Congregational, "His wife just up and left him one day with no message or anything. The next time Matthew Douglas heard from her was when he got the papers saying she and the Reverend weren't compatible." Mildred had knowingly announced this bit of information to a group of girls over lunch one day at The Diner at the Docks.

"Of course, you know how some churches are when their preachers are having problems," she had expounded. "They sure want the preacher to be available when *they* need *him*, but they can't seem to be around when he needs them back. And don't you know, that big, fancy church in Dallas just couldn't find it in their hearts to do anything but ask our good Reverend to move on. Can you believe it? 'Course that might have been the best thing anyway, with him being a country boy and all. I say he's better off here with people who appreciate him. But, I'm telling you I think he's still mighty broken up about that wife of his. When I'm up at the church seeing about things, you know, sometimes I notice him just staring out the window with a real sad look, like he thinks she's just going to come walking up the street at any minute." Leaning in closer to the group, she lowered her voice and looked to the right, then the left before continuing.

"Now, I'm not swearin' to this, and if you say it came from me, I'll say you're lyin', but a little birdie told me that his wife just up and died right before the good Reverend moved away."

Remembering Mildred's dialogue, Libbie found herself sympathizing with, as well as respecting Matt even more, knowing that he had to not only tolerate, but also appease the Mildred Vickerys of the world. Following her train of thought, she said, "Matt, you shouldn't have sent me anything, but it was certainly very thoughtful of you. I hope that the people in your congregation have realized how very fortunate they are."

Turning to answer the door again, she realized that Matt, like Vince Morgan, had also been holding her hand as they talked. Funny, it didn't seem to bother her this time.

She introduced Matt to Paula and Zach Henderson, owners of Henderson Furniture, who were followed by Shelley and Jimbo, running up the walk. Aunt Emma had always claimed that Shelley never let any grass grow under her feet, and Libbie did often find it hard to keep up with her.

"Hi everyone. Hope we're not late," Shelley said, breathlessly. "Jimbo and I have worked all day at the docks trying to salvage one of his boats that was damaged by the tornado, and just straightening up some of the mess around the place. Now I know why it takes him so long to get cleaned up every evening," she said, rolling her eyes at Jimbo and grinning. "For the first time since he started the charter business, I think that I actually smelled worse than he did today!" As usual, Shelley brought joy and laughter with her, and as the little group headed toward the living room, Libbie cautiously entertained the thought that the evening did, indeed, seem to be off to a good start.

Chapter 6

A friend is a gift you give yourself.
Robert Louis Stevenson

Couples Supper Club had been meeting together for nine years, a record which made the charter members quite proud. The original founders had been Libbie and Rob, Shelley and Jimbo, Rob's partner Neal Roper and his wife, Nancy, Zach and Paula Henderson, Bob and Vicki, and George and Fran Greenburg, owners of and partners in the law firm of Greenburg and Cohen. Cohen was Fran's maiden name, and she had been insistent that it be part of the firm's name. Never mind that Cohen followed Greenburg. "It just means that I have the last word," she had joked when the sign had gone up in front of their newly remodeled offices in the old brick warehouse district overlooking the panoramic Apalachicola River.

The group had grown slightly over the years to include Kerri Graham, one of the town's most beloved first grade teachers, and her husband Buddy, a contractor. In addition, they generally tried to include guests such as family members or new people in the community.

Traditionally the supper club met once every three months in a different home, with the members bringing everything but the meat and drinks, which were supplied by the hostess. At least once a year they went out to eat in Tallahassee or Panama City, neither more than a ninety-minute drive.

They usually had a short meeting to discuss current business or community concerns, and they had found that the best time to do so was right before the meal. They had tried waiting until after dinner, but inevitably someone would have to leave early, or they would be so full, that all they cared about at that point was going home to bed.

"It's certainly not our age," they had joked. "It must be the good cooking."

At 7:45 Libbie decided that they should start the meeting, even though the Greenburgs had not arrived. As Jimbo passed by on his way to get seconds, maybe thirds of Paula's crab dip, Libbie grabbed his arm and asked him to help her get everyone seated. Then, without warning, a sharp - almost physical pang of melancholy stabbed her as she remembered Rob calling the group together several years ago in this very room. She quickly excused herself from the room, muttering something about checking on the oven. In the kitchen, she closed her eyes and took several deep breaths.

"OK, God, here I am, asking for help again," she prayed. "Maybe I wasn't ready for this yet. Have I been fooling myself? It's been a year and a half now, and You know how hard I've tried....but just when things seem to be getting easier, something like this happens!"

Taking another deep breath, she said to herself, as much as to God, "All right, I've been here before; I know I can - no, WE can do this. Those people out there in that room are the best friends a person could have, and I'm so thankful for them. I'll just concentrate on that..."

Opening her eyes, she couldn't help but smile when they focused on the refrigerator magnet right in front of her. For once, she was even thankful for one of Aunt Emma's catalogue purchases, this one a picture of two little girls sharing an ice cream cone above a caption which simply read, "Friends are God's way of loving us through others."

As if on cue, Aunt Emma came shuffling into the kitchen, her slow movement an indication to Libbie that the balmy, stormy weather that morning had taken a toll on her arthritis.

"Libbie, I think they're waiting on you to start the meeting," Emmaline said. "You go on in there with your company now, and I'll keep a watch on the rolls."

"Oh, thanks Emmy. But I'll only go if you promise to sit at the table and wait for the buzzer instead of bustling around looking for something to do. Everything else is ready, and you just need to put the rolls in that basket when they're done. That will be a tremendous help. In fact, I don't know what I would do without you."

"Well, hello and goodbye, girl! Isn't that what I've been telling you for years? Now, go on, put a smile on that pretty face and make yourself proud."

Dear Aunt Emma – talk about perception. She just always seemed to appear when Libbie needed her most.

Jimbo Hopkins was standing by the fireplace when Libbie entered the room. Everyone else was seated, and Jimbo motioned her to the empty arm chair next to him.

"Come on, Lib. We can't begin this meeting without you, and we're getting hungry. You don't mind that I sort of took over and got things started do you?"

Thank God for Jimbo. When they wrote the book about good old southern boys, Jimbo could have been the role model. If he wasn't out running a fishing charter, he could usually be found around town in his white extended cab pick-up truck with his yellow lab puppies, Winston and Elvis, riding in the back. Like Jimmy Johns, he always had a baseball cap on, but his was always blue, with a smiling University of Florida gator on it. Jimbo was seldom seen without a smile as wide as the gator's.

Unlike Jimmy Johns, Jimbo had been a very bright, inquisitive student in the Apalachicola Public Schools, but his grades had been less than exciting. Teachers today would have labeled him with Attention Deficit Disorder; his teachers of yesteryear had simply assumed that he was too interested in other things like hunting, fishing, girls, and football, not necessarily in that order. His mother had understood better than anyone that her son was fascinated with everything that the world around him had to offer, and he just didn't have the time to waste on learning about it through someone else's eyes.

"My boy has the gift of an exploring spirit, and he has more love and devotion than most folks. He will go just as far in life as he and the good Lord have a mind for him to go!" she had said, defending Jimbo time and time again during his school years. And, as predicted, Jimbo had become one of the town's most succesful and adored citizens.

Libbie gave him an appreciative smile and said, "Not at all, Jimbo. In fact, keep right on. The floor is all yours."

"Okay; well, first, I know that we all want to thank Libbie for having us tonight," Jimbo drawled in his easy, no-nonsense way.

Thanks were immediately forthcoming from around the room, and Jimbo, cautiously aware of Libbie's fragile emotions, probably because Shelley had warned him earlier, wisely moved on to the other business at hand.

"Now the only announcements that I know of are about Neal and Nancy's trip, and the treasurer's report. I guess you all know that the Ropers are on their Yucatan Cruise, and I'm sure that we are the farthest things from their minds tonight. But, Nancy did want us to remind you that they will have supper club next time, in August, and it's going to be some kind of Mexican pile-up stuff, so she'll tell you what to bring when she gets back with all of her new recipes.

"And by the way, Fran and George are going to be late tonight, because they've been in Tallahassee checking on Fran's inheritance. Hey, but Libbie was on the ball, and she assigned them the dessert to bring in case they miss the main meal.

"So now I guess I'll pass the treasury basket and—"

"Psst - Jimbo," Shelley interrupted. "You forgot to welcome our guests."

"Oh, yeah. I'm sorry. I guess you've all met the Morgans and Reverend Matthew by now. And everybody knows Ms. Emma; she's practically a standing member of the group. Hey, we're glad you all could join us, and we hope you'll come again," he said. "And you visitors, don't feel like you have to add anything to the treasury basket unless you want to. It's just a little something we do to be good neighbors and help out in the community when we can."

Matt smiled and nodded, dropping $10.00 in the basket as it went by. He handed it to Vince Morgan next to him who put in a dollar and passed it on.

"Shelley tells me that right now we've got around $500.00 in the treasury," Jimbo continued. "Last month we sent a fruit basket to Andy Jenkins over at the newspaper when his mother died. And we sent our normal monthly donation to Jason Mitchell at the seminary out in Fort Worth. But it seems like we've got a little more than usual left over right now. Does anyone have a request or know of a need?"

Keri Graham raised her hand like one of her first graders might do.

"Buddy and I would like to suggest that we help Chris and Sylvia Patronis with the Diner at the Docks. They were hit pretty badly today by the tornado. It looks like they can't even open back up until they get the front eating area rebuilt."

"Yeah, I've been over there this afternoon making some notes to give them an estimate on material costs," Buddy Graham said. "I told them I would do the work for cost, to assure a quick re-opening. You know I can't go long without my vegetables for lunch everyday, and Keri's already informed me that she's not going to cook them for me."

Amid light-hearted laughter someone asked what they needed most.

"Well, let me tell you what I saw first-hand over there today," Libbie offered. "I had asked Sylvia to cook my lamb roast for tonight, and I went to pick it up this afternoon. Bless her heart, she had cooked it at home for me, since her ovens were down at the diner. Anyway, I'm afraid that I had been so busy getting ready for tonight, that I had not even glanced at the paper when Jimmy brought it to me. So, I had no idea that the diner had been hit. And Keri's right; all of the front room things like tables, chairs, cloths, curtains, and pictures are ruined. I think the wall booths are still intact, but they appeared to be slightly damaged also."

For the first time all evening, Claire Morgan seemed to come alive. "Vince and I have two round oak tables that were my mother's, and they don't match anything at all in our beach house. We could let them use those," she offered in a somewhat hesitant voice. Libbie noticed that she seemed to intentionally, almost defiantly, avoid her husband's startled stare.

Joining in the spirit of benevolence, Matt remembered an attic full of old oak chairs that the church had used before the purchase of pews.

"I would have to get the church's approval, of course, but I know that most of the members frequent the diner, so I can't imagine that there would be any objections," he said.

"You know, we have some old sturdy wooden card tables at the Inn that are just used as folding tables in the laundry room now," Shelley chimed in. "We could spare a few of those, don't you think, Jimbo?" Without waiting for his answer, she added, "But we would need to buy some table cloths to cover the cigarette burns and glass stains."

Paula Henderson remembered some bolts of gingham chintz that someone had ordered at the furniture store years ago and had never picked up. "They're in the warehouse still wrapped in plastic," she said. "There's even an extra bolt of coordinating floral material that we could include. They would make darling curtains and cloths for the tables."

The enthusiasm was contagious and most of those present, hunger temporarily forgotten, were ready to jump right in to the re-building of the diner - until George and Fran walked into the room.

"Hey guys, hold on a minute," George called from the doorway. "Fran and I heard your plans as we were letting ourselves in just now, and it sounds like the decision to help Chris and Sylvia is unanimous. But don't you think that we better ask them what they would like? We could offer everything that's been mentioned, but they just might prefer hands-on help, or just money."

Jimbo walked over and shook hands with his friend. "Hey man. It's about time you two lawyers got here to keep us straight. You know, since the rest of us had the idea," he said, "why don't you and Fran find out what Chris and Sylvia would like for us to do? Is that okay with everyone?" Hearing murmurs of approval, Jimbo continued. "Now, are there any more concerns?"

Buddy brought them up to date on the damage at Soloman and Ella Horton's Meat Market. The store, which Soloman's grandfather had established during World War 1, was one of the most prosperous home-owned business in the village, and was a landmark on The Hill, a well-respected, predominately black area of town. Buddy suggested that they could probably best help Soloman and Ella if they went and bought up as much of the meat as possible.

"They just need some windows replaced and a new roof, which I'm going to do for them at cost also. But that place was a mess inside when I was there this morning. They were without electricity and Ms. Ella was real worried about food spoiling." Buddy chuckled as he recalled his conversation with the couple.

"Y'all should have heard Soloman and Ella carrying on like they do. Big Soloman was rubbing his elbow and saying that his bones were telling him there's a 'heap more trouble coming on this town,' and Ms. Ella was telling him to hush up and get busy - and to quit acting like his Auntie Mae, claiming to predict the future with his body parts. Those two can always make me grin, even when things look as bad as they did today."

"Hey, I have a big generator at the docks that they can use." Jimbo offered. "I'll check on them tomorrow and see if they need anything else. Now, if it's all right with the rest of you, I move that we close this meeting."

Robert's Rules of Order were foreign to their informal meetings, and a simple yes or nod of the head was generally enough to count as an official vote. Jimbo noted the approval of the members and Bob Callaway followed his move to close with a quick "I second that; let's eat. I've been hungry ever since Libbie mentioned Sylvia's roast."

"No problem here," said Jimbo. "Reverend, would you bless the meal for us?"

"Of course," Matt replied. "Let's bow our heads."

> "Father, for the food we are about receive and
> for the hands that prepared it, we thank You,
> in Jesus' name,
> Amen."

Bob was already the first one up, having risen before the blessing. Leading the line towards the dining room, he remarked to his wife, Vicki, "Hey Hon, I liked that blessing; short, sweet and to the point. I just might have to visit that preacher's church one of these days."

"Yeah, right," Vicki mumbled.

Chapter 7

Some anglers catch their best fish by the "tale."
Old fisherman's saying - source unknown

The food, as always, was delicious and conversation easy as the group dined casually on lap trays in the den. They were all anxious to hear about Fran's visit to Tallahassee, where she had been making inquiries through an international accountancy firm which was handling the dormant Swiss accounts of Holocaust victims. And Fran had, indeed, received some very promising news that very afternoon.

"You all might remember me telling you that my family lived with my grandparents before the war. My grandfather was a well-respected doctor in Germany, and when the soldiers came, they took him away first. They soon came back for the rest of us, and my sister and I ended up in a camp completely separated from our other family members. We were quite small, and I don't remember too much about it, but I do know that I never saw my parents, brother, or grandparents again. I did hear that my grandfather had been allowed to medically treat some wounded guards in one of the camps, but I was never able to confirm the truth of the story or the name of the camp.

"When my sister and I were released at the end of the war, our cousin, David, found us and managed to bring us to the states where he took care of our upbringing. He always talked about the money that 'Grumpappa' had put away somewhere. Well, friends, it appears that our story is finally going to have a happy ending. The accountant's representative told me today that Grandfather's account has been identified, and Julie and I are the sole beneficiaries, since our cousin, David, recently passed away. George and I have already decided that we will spend some of it on the re-furbishing of the warehouses. We are thrilled to be able to give something back to this special little community that has meant so much to us."

The Greenburgs had moved to Apalachicola from Pensacola three years earlier. They had bought the lovely Cawthon mansion across the street from the bay, and, with the help of a professional Historical Architect and an Interior Decorator from Atlanta, they had restored it to its original splendor which had certainly pleased the long-standing locals. They had also bought several of the dilapidated brick cotton warehouses by the river, and after re-modeling one for their offices, had begun making plans to re-furbish the three others to be used as stores, offices and an occasional apartment.

Everyone was full of questions for Fran, and Aunt Emma, who couldn't hear most of the conversation anyway, excused herself to go plug in the coffee just as the phone rang in the kitchen.

* * *

It was not unusual for Jimbo Hopkins to regale an audience with "remember when" stories and, back in the den, the menu had inspired him to recall one of his more colorful tales.

"Hey y'all, Sylvia's gravy here reminds me of the football game our senior year when we played that team from Central," he said. "Do you remember that game, Bubba? It was in September when some hurricane was threatening the Gulf Coast, but those inland guys didn't have a clue about how bad things could get, and they insisted on playing the game instead of canceling it until the next weekend. Anyway, so, hey, we were up for it"

"Yeah, are you talking about the game that was canceled during half-time?" Bubba asked.

"That's the one," Jimbo said with a mischievous grin, "and most of you probably think it was canceled because of the weather, right? Well, I'm gonna tell y'all something that probably none of you know except maybe Bubba, and I swear it's the truth," Jimbo said, holding his right hand up in the air as if giving testimony in a court room, and almost knocking his glass of tea over.

"Jimbo, calm down and be more careful," Shelley scolded.

"OK, Babe, but this is so funny I can't help it."

"Now it all started with the opening kick-off. The wind was already so strong that the ref had to toss the coin a second time just to catch it. I promise I ain't lyin. Anyway, Central won the toss and chose to kick.

"So, picture this now. The kicker, he huffs and puffs and paws the ground like some old bull getting ready to charge, and then he comes at that ball full steam, and just when his foot connects with the ball, a strong gust of wind makes him lose his balance. Man, he fell flat on the ground - didn't hurt much except his pride, but the funniest thing was what the ball did. It just went a little way forward, then straight up in the air before it blew backwards about twenty feet. The referee ruled that it was a completed kick, and we got the ball on their 30-yard line. We scored on the very next play when the wind carried Bruce's pass right to Skipper Jones in the end zone. Of course they were yelling unfair home team advantage by then. Yeah, like we had some kind of control over the wind or something.

"Well, they kept on 'til they made ol' Paxton Brice madder than....well, you folks know how mad he can get. So anyway, right before half-time, he went over to the fence where his little brother was eating some roast beef that his mom had fixed for him in one of those little plastic containers; she was always trying to firm those boys up. Anyway, ol' Paxton, he poured himself a mouthful of his momma's gravy, and on the next play when he lined up, he spit a stream of that gravy through that space between his two front teeth, right into the eyes of some big ol' guard across from him. He did it right when the ball was snapped, so nobody really saw him except," Jimbo stopped at this point to catch his breath from laughing, "that guard who went yelpin' off the field like a whipped puppy. We figured there musta been some powerful garlic in that gravy!

"Well, you probably know the rest of the story. The coaches had a big meeting right there on the field, and everybody was making accusations, and nobody could prove nuthin'. So, the refs just decided to call the game on account of the weather."

"Aw come on man," Zach called out. "That's one of your biggest stories yet. Are you sure you didn't stretch this one a little bit just to entertain our guests here? Hey, Matt and the Morgans, they don't know you as well as we do."

"Did someone say the Morgans? Aunt Emma called from the kitchen door. "Hmm, maybe that's who the phone was for. I thought they said Jordans, and I told them they had the wrong number."

Chapter 8

*May the great God between your shoulder
blades protect you in your going and returning.*
Old Irish Blessing

"Mom! Oh, Mom," Trish sobbed over the phone. "I hate to interrupt your party, but something pretty bad has happened."

Libbie's hand froze on the receiver, and her blood ran cold at the frantic sound of her daughter's voice.

"Oh, please God, let my babies be all right," she quickly prayed.

"Trish, honey, calm down and tell me what's wrong. Where are you? Where is Travis?"

"We're both okay, Mom; just a little shaken up is all," Trish said, unconvincingly. "Hold on; I'm going to let Wes tell you —"

"Trish, wait," Libbie called into the phone.

"Hello, Mrs. Whitestone? Hi, this is Wes."

"Yes, I know, Wes. Just tell me what's happened!"

"Well, we're all okay, but Travis and Rachel have been taken to the Medical Center for a check-up, and just for precaution."

"Oh, my gosh, Wes. Were y'all in a wreck?"

"No, ma'am. It's really weird, and I can't explain it all on the phone right now, but someone banged Travis and Rachel up pretty badly. It looks like they came up on a robbery attempt at Rachel's house.

"The ambulance just left, and we told Sheriff Coggins that we would call you. He's already tried to reach the Morgans, but he got the wrong number or something, so we said that we would be sure they found out. Can you tell them what's happened please? Trish and I are in the car now on our way to the medical center. Why don't you meet us there? And Mrs. Whitestone, don't worry, they're going to be fine."

Wes' deep, reassuring voice brought the hot, stinging tears to Libbie's eyes that she had fought back since answering the phone. As she hung up, strong hands took hold of her shoulders and firmly ushered her to the nearest chair.

"Come on Libbie; have a seat and tell me what's wrong," Jimbo said.

A host of pent-up emotions, ones which had been neatly packed away in the small, dark corners of her mind, welled up inside of her and threatened to burst open. She tried to talk, but could only gulp, as she made the attempt to gain control of herself.

Shelley knelt beside her and squeezed her hand. "Lib, I heard your part of the conversation. Just tell me; are the kids okay?"

Libbie took one of her well-rehearsed breaths and found her voice, shaky but sufficient enough to tell what little she knew.

"Okay, kiddo. We'll take it from here," Jimbo said in his gentle but firm way.

Libbie, Shelley, and Jimbo left immediately for the medical center, with the Morgans following closely behind. Vicki and Fran stayed to serve the dessert and act as hostesses for the remaining friends, who also wanted to know what they could do.

"Please, just stay and enjoy yourselves," Libbie urged. "Maybe we won't be too long."

Matt promised to stay with Aunt Emma until Libbie returned, no matter what the time.

Shelley fussed at Jimbo to slow down as he sped through the neighborhood, turning to take a short-cut down a quaint little avenue running toward town. Small, frame cottage-style row houses, once homes for the cotton mill workers, lined the sidewalks on either side of the avenue, and huge, old live oaks formed a canopy across much of the street. Their limbs were draped with Spanish moss, lending a secluded and often eerie atmosphere to the little street after sundown.

The neighborhood had been re-zoned commercial in the seventies, and most of the little houses had quickly become re-modeled doctor's offices, artist studios, gift shops, and antique stores. In fact, only one property owner, Mr. Winston Stoudamire, still lived in his home on the short street. He had refused to sell out when all of his neighbors had "grabbed their money and run," and few had ever complained. After all, his yard was immaculate, and he took pride in displaying the prettiest rose and hydrangea beds in town. At peak season, he took pleasure in adorning the lobbies of the doctor's offices with his generous bouquets.

Despite his generosity, he was often referred to as the Monster of Mill Street due, in part, to his crooked body and gruff voice. In addition, his disposition had grown quite temperamental with age, and he had little patience with youngsters who picked his flowers or threw trash in his yard. On more than one occasion he had chased mischevious kids from his yard shaking his walking cane at them and threatening to call the police.

Libbie briefly glanced at the large front window of The Yellow Canary, a unique little gift shop housed in a quaint, mustard-yellow, gingerbread-style cottage with green-striped awnings over the windows. She noticed that one of her own paintings, which featured small children collecting shells by the seashore, was still the focal point of the window's colorful beach-theme display.

She wistfully thought of the enlarged snapshot on her dresser at home - the picture that Rob had taken so many years ago of Travis and Trish at the beach in their little matching polka-dot bathing suits and beach hats. Her oil painting in the gift shop window had been inspired by the cherished snapshot and was one of her favorite pieces of work. In fact, she had refused to sell the painting several times, and the manager of The Yellow Canary understood that the picture was on loan for display purposes only, as representation of Libbie's work.

The thought that those same precious twins, now practically grown, were in a hospital just moments down the street, triggered within her a staggering jolt of reality - the frightening acknowledgment that she could no longer hold their hands and kiss the "boo-boos" to make them well. She struggled to control the maternal instinct to protect her children from the dangers of the world, and she concentrated hard on the comforting vision of a Heavenly Father holding them in the palms of His hands. Yet, the urge to wrap her arms around them was fierce at the moment.

The Medical Center lit up the right side of the street with a welcoming glow. The circular drive leading to the front entrance was lined with palm trees which lent a casual, homelike atmosphere to the one-story brick building, Construction was presently underway on a new five-story wing off the back of the original building which would house, among other things, a rehabilitation center.

Jimbo's long truck whined as he maneuvered it into a corner parking space in the back lot behind the emergency wing. He mumbled something about some of the hospital money being spent on creating some decent size spaces for people to park larger vehicles.

"Not everybody drives one of those little foreign numbers," he complained, as he checked the space between his truck and the car next to him to make sure the car's occupants weren't close enough to put a door-ding in his truck.

"Oh hush your grumbling," Shelley chastised, grabbing him by the arm and urging him to hurry, as she glanced to her left, where Libbie was already meeting the Morgan's car. "That's not what Libbie and the Morgans need to hear right now," she whispered.

The E.R. lobby of the Big Bend Medical Center was unusually empty for a Friday night. A young girl dressed in cut-off jeans, an over-sized T-shirt and scruffy bedroom slippers sat in the corner soothing her congested baby, whose little face was welped from crying. The apparent father, a lanky young man whose unkempt appearance suggested little recent sleep, was beating on the coke machine next to her in a fit of anger over the loss of his money. The wide-eyed attempts of the frustrated young mother to calm the man down seemed futile, causing the matronly, stone-face nurse at the reception desk to look up from her crossword puzzle with a disapproving glance in their direction.

The only other person in the waiting room was Sheriff Coggins who was pacing the floor and drinking a cup of coffee. When the group arrived, he hurried toward the door and started to explain what he had found.

"Begging your pardon, Bernie," Jimbo cut in, "but I think these parents are a little anxious to see their kids first. Why don't you show us where they are, and you can tell us what happened while we walk. By the way, have you met the Morgans here?"

"No, I haven't," Bernie replied. "And I'm sorry to meet you under these circumstances, but folks, it looks like things are going to be just fine. It could have been a lot worse, you know.

"Come on and I'll take you back to their rooms. I think they've both suffered mild concussions, and Travis is kind of black and blue in places, but he's 'chompin' at the bit' to go home. Turning to the Morgans he added, "That pretty little girl of yours has a nasty bump on her head, and Doc might want to keep her overnight for observation. But all in all, I'd say those two are mighty lucky."

It appeared that Aunt Emma had every light in the house on when the weary Whitestones arrived home around twelve fifteen. Libbie was so grateful to Matt for staying. That had been one less thing to worry about, and she gave him a warm, if rather limp, hug when she walked in the door.

True to her nature, Emmaline Harris, upon determining that her niece and the twins were all right, promptly marched everyone upstairs to bed. She still had the stamina to take charge in a crisis, even if her efforts were less forceful than they used to be.

Walking Matthew to the door, she said, "Now son, you'll join us for a late breakfast in the morning, won't you? Say around ten oclock? I'll fix some eggs and grits and some of that country ham that my brother-in-law sends me from Tennessee. I save it for special occasions, you know, and I certainly think that hearing all about tonight's activities will qualify as a special occasion.

"Thanks so much for staying with me. It's not everyday that I have a good-looking man all to myself! Oh, and Matthew, never mind about that phone call. Let's don't even mention it. I probably just misunderstood what that man said anyway. So, good night."

"Good night, Mrs. Harris. You lock up tight now," Matt called, trying not to sound as apprehensive as he felt.

"No ma'am," he thought as he walked down the sidewalk. *"You didn't misunderstand anything."* Earlier in the evening, Matt had picked up the phone in the den just as a voice had said, "I'm in big trouble, ma'am. I really need to see you." The line had gone dead when Mrs. Harris had failed to respond.

Chapter 9

Patience is bitter, but its fruit is sweet.
Jean Jacques Rousseau

Summer arrived like a ferocious dragon, blowing its hot, fiery breath over the bay area. The weather reports had been boringly repetitious for days with lows in the high 70s and highs in the upper 90s. The elevated humidity caused the heat index to hover between 105-110 degrees. There was an appeasing hint of afternoon thunder showers - no more than 30% chance daily - which some said was nature's own way of screaming "Enough"!

No one was more aware of its hot, sticky presence than Wes and Travis, who were doing summer construction work with Buddy Graham's company between their spring and fall school quarters. Buddy had them working on the building repairs for Horton's Meat and Grocery, a task which was made considerably easier and more enjoyable with help from Soloman, when Ms. Ella could spare him.

One particularly hot Friday a few weeks after the island escapade, Travis put down his hammer and stopped for a break. "Whew-ee, Big Soloman! Thank goodness you've got these trees here to give us a little shade. I don't think I could stand working that other job of Mr. Graham's out on the island in the blazing sun," Travis said as he re-adjusted his red and white bandanna to loosely cover the hospital bandage over his right eye. Doc had warned him to keep the area as dry as possible, a rather impossible feat in the stifling heat.

"Boy, you're looking mighty hot to me..." Soloman called back. "You know your mama and your auntie ain't gonna let you work if you go an' get yourself sick, now. And my Ella - boys, she'll skin us all alive an' fry us for dinner if we ain't careful out here."

Soloman sat down and patted the ground next to a tall pine tree. "You boys come on over here an' rest a spell. I've got some of Ella's ice tea in this jug, and she sent along some extra cups."

"Gee, thanks, Soloman. I'd never turn down Ms. Ella's sweet tea. It is sweet, isn't it?" Wes called as he climbed down the ladder from the roof.

Travis and Wes splashed water on their faces from the nearby hose on the side of the building and went to join Soloman, who wanted to know first-hand about their island escapade.

"Some of the guys at the docks was sayin' that somebody hit you on the head, Travis, an' tied you up in the garage with the dog."

"Yeah, poor little fellow," Travis said. "That little puppy was banged up pretty bad. He wasn't even conscious when I first saw him. He's okay now, though. Doc Hastings said he had a few broken ribs, and a punctured lung. He said somebody must have been pretty angry to beat up on the little fellow like that."

"What about the girl?" Soloman asked.

"Rachel? Yeah, she's okay too. She tried to run when she came up and saw the guy pulling me into the garage. Man, I was out cold. Apparently he saw her and just shoved me on down the steps into the garage, so he could go after her. Hey, I'm sportin' some pretty good bruises to prove it, see?"

He pulled up the right side of his T-shirt, revealing a nasty looking purple rib area.

"Anyway, the dude chased her, and it looks like he clobbered her on the back of the head when he caught up to her. Then he must have picked her up and dumped her up in the sand dunes. Nice guy, huh? You better believe I'm looking for him."

"Yeah, a bunch of us guys are after the freak," Wes offered. "If he's stupid enough to still be around, we figure we'll find him faster than ol' Bernie Cog does. Heck, he's too busy worrying about cleaning up and stuff, anyway.

"Did I tell you that he's still on our case about the bonfire? It seems we didn't cover our tracks, so to speak, by going back and putting the fire out. You know, it was such a crummy fire, that I wasn't very worried about it. And Trish and I did have more important things on our mind, like people we cared about who had just been hauled off in an ambulance. Ol' Bernie said that we could have set the whole end of the island on fire. He threatened to fine us and everything. Can you believe that guy?"

"Well, boys, I know it sounds crazy of the sheriff to carry on like that and all, but it's part of his job, too, you know," Soloman broke in. "And besides, I think he's really more worried than you think about catching that burglar. I hear the guy took some of Mrs. Morgan's jewelry, and there's been some other reports of thievin' on the island lately, too." Big Soloman pulled out a white, crisply ironed handkerchief and wiped his forehead.

"Me and Ella been talkin' about how you kids was sure protected by the Lord that night. Yes, sir, as my papa used to say, 'The Lord just swooped you up in his big ol' hands and held you tight.' Now you boys ought not to go pressin' your luck, when you're riding so high in the lap of the Lord's luxury. Seems to me you might as well just let the Sheriff do his sheriffin' job, and you boys stay out of it."

"Sure, like the job he's done finding my dad's killer," Travis sneered as he spit out a lemon seed.

"Come on now, Travis. That ain't fair. You know there ain't nobody wants to solve that case more than Sheriff Coggins. Why, he and your papa was good friends, huntin' buddies and all. He's even been workin' real close with those guys who came up here all the way from Miami this week," Soloman reminded him.

"What guys?" Wes asked.

"Trish hasn't told you?" Travis once again adjusted the bandanna that kept slipping down over his eye. "Well, it looks like Dad might have accidentally stumbled onto a big drug delivery when he was hunting that morning near the old abandoned Turner airstrip. That's who those dudes were driving that black Volvo in town yesterday...some narcs from down state. Funny thing to me is that Dad and ol' Bernie Cog were supposed to be hunting together the morning he was killed.

"Oh well, this isn't getting the job done," Travis said suddenly as he jumped up, a little too fast for Soloman's mind. Soloman remembered only too well being that age - 'antsy' his grandmother had called him - constantly searching, easily dissatisfied, and always ready to blame someone else when things didn't seem quite right.

Chapter 10

Loneliness wouldn't be so hard to fight if I didn't have to do it by myself.

Thoreau

Out on St. George Island, Trish Whitestone, like her brother, was also bemoaning the heat, thankful that today was Friday, and she was about to have two days break from the sun. Being out in the open most of the day had initially produced a great tan, but by mid-June, she had to take Aunt Emma's advice and wear number 25 protective sunscreen daily, along with a baseball hat she had borrowed from Wes to hold back her ponytail and shield her face.

She considered herself very fortunate to be doing research for the Department of Environmental Protection, Natural Estaurine Reserve. Not only did she get credit hours toward her Biology major, but the experience was incredible!

Her job involved the research and study of the nesting / birth activities of the endangered loggerhead turtles. Each summer, starting in June, these large sea turtles made their way up onto the beaches to make their nests and lay their eggs. Their nesting practices extended through July and August, and the babies who hatched at varying intervals were counted and observed as closely as possible.

The government was very protective of these babies from such threats as animal predators, human curiosity, carelessness, and sadly, intentional malice. In fact, just recently, Trish had found five nests that had been purposely destroyed, the eggs smashed and the protective roping around the nests ripped apart.

A new concern was the recent rise in disorientation among some of the babies themselves, who, upon birth, were making their way towards the lights of the beaches rather than following their natural inclination toward the water. Ordinarily, no more than two to three cases of disorientation per year were reported, but this year, for some unknown reason, during the first two weeks of hatching, at least twenty cases had been documented. Part of Trish's job was to figure out why and try to remedy the situation.

Trish set about daily to locate as many new nests as possible, rope them off, and put out signs to educate the public about the turtle's activities. In addition, she had drawn up informative fliers to be placed in stores and real estate offices. Her most challenging responsibility, however, was the observation of the babies when they actually hatched, which was usually at night. When possible, she recorded their actions, the time involved, and on occasion, sneaked a picture or two with a special camera. Spending so much time with her work at night had threatened to interfere with her time to be with Wes.

"Hey Sassy, do you think I'm going to let you roam those beaches alone at night, especially after what happened to us? No way, girl. We'll just find those little baby boogers together," Wes had assured her. And true to his word, he had become a supportive, even interested turtle watcher.

After a long, hot afternoon of working on the roof of Horton's Market, Wes joined Trish out on the island around dusk. Trish was writing up the last of her reports for the day when Wes noticed a lone baby turtle straggling toward the street light. He cupped his giant hands together and formed a wall in front of the newborn. Gently he coaxed the baby around and gave it a nudge toward the ocean, watching, satisfied, as its natural instincts took over.

"Okay, Sassy, mission accomplished. Now let's go join Travis and Rachel at her place." He said, grinning as he stood up, obviously pleased with his accomplishment.

"Not yet, big guy. Come over here for a minute. We have one more thing to do." Trish called.

Wes headed toward the car, where Trish was writing in her notebook. She tore out the last sheet and handed it to him with a pen.

"You just have to read and sign this." She said with a mischievous smile.

As Wes read the sheet, a grin spread across his face. "Whoa, Sassy," he said. "No problem here."

Reaching out for Trish, he gently surrounded her with his huge, sun-bronzed arms and kissed the top of her blonde head. No words were necessary as the two of them stood in the evening breeze, aware of only each other.

A young man slinked behind a car across the street and smirked.

"Aw, just look at them two lovebirds. That's sickening. I guess they're so wrapped up in each other they don't even know what the real world is like....yeah, my world. Too bad; I'd be glad to tell them about it. Course, I don't know what their world is like either. Must be nice, all comfortable and full of people hugging on you and all.

"Hey, I wonder what I would have to do for somebody like one of them to love me like that. One thing's for sure, slugging that dude on the head and pushing him down the stairs probably didn't make me one of their favorite people. Oh well, you do what you've gotta do in my world.

"Yeah, and she's one of them; I'm not too sure she would love me now, either. I know she'd say she was disappointed in me. But, hey, she just doesn't know what it was like. I tried to tell her that time, when I went to her house, but she had that company and told me to come back later. Well, now it's later, and it's about time....

"Aw, who am I kidding? Ain't nobody ever going to love me. I don't know why I'm wasting my time even thinking about it. Yeah, it's just me against the world now, and I better get busy doing something about it. Looks like even Scotty ain't going to come through for me no more.

"Oh well, I better go climb in the back of that big dude's truck while he's playing kissy-poo with blondie. I hope they don't mess around out here on the island for too long tonight. I need to get back into town, maybe hit one or two joints out on 98 before too late. Seems like I remembered Scotty having a buddy or two out there. Maybe I ought to check with that Bubbles broad at the Top Flite Lounge and Grill. Yeah, she put me in touch with Scotty in the first place. Heck, I need me a little female company anyway."

* * *

The obnoxious sound of Travis' horn jerked Wes and Trish back to reality.

"Hey, you two; we got tired of waiting for you. How much longer are you going to be?" Travis called out of the driver's window of his Jeep.

"We're about to wrap it up," Trish called. "Where are you going?"

"Some of the people that Rachel works with at the Inn are having a party on the island. Why don't y'all come go with us?" Travis answered.

Wes quickly spoke for both of them. "Thanks, but we have a little more to do here. Maybe we'll join you guys later. Y'all go on and have a good time."

Travis honked as he and Rachel drove off. "Those two aren't even thinking about joining us," he said.

"Probably not," Rachel thought. *"Actually, I kind of envy them."*

She and Travis had become close friends in the last month, but that seemed to be all. He was unusually nice, fun and affectionate, with looks to die for - tall and thin with curly, dark-brown hair and his mother's green eyes. Her parents seemed to like him well enough...all the ingredients for the perfect guy. But there was a reserve about him that seemed to stand in the way of their relationship developing further. Maybe he had a girl back at school. Maybe he just wasn't ready for any kind of commitment. Well, she certainly didn't have to push for one. There were plenty of guys waiting for her return to Miami in the fall.

Chapter 11

Honesty is the first chapter in the book of wisdom.
Thomas Jefferson

"A penny for your thoughts, girl," Travis coaxed, reaching over to pull Rachel closer.

"Funny that you should mention it," she ventured. "But now that we're on the subject, it's probably a good time to tell you exactly what I was thinking. Actually, I was wondering what it is that seems to preoccupy YOUR thoughts so much of the time. I mean, just like earlier tonight. You came in at the house and had a great conversation with Mom and Dad. Then, when you and I went out on the porch, you just sort of clammed up. I tried to talk to you about your mom's art display in the lobby at the Hopkins House. I asked about your job, your headaches, when your fraternity rush starts, and just about everything else I could think of to talk about. All you did was give me one-liners back. Then, all of a sudden, you jump up and say, 'Let's get out of here and go find Wes and Trish.' You know, Travis, I kind of feel like someone who's just along for the ride."

Travis shifted uncomfortably in his seat, slowed the car down, and pulled over in front of a vacant beach house. Avoiding Rachel's eyes, he stared straight ahead, both hands tightly clutching the steering wheel. "I'm sorry, Rachel. I haven't been completely fair with you, I guess. It's just that it's really hard for me to open up about certain things."

"That's okay, Travis; I don't want to push you to talk about anything that makes you uncomfortable, but it might do you good sometimes. Something's obviously bothering you, and if it's something that you ever want to talk about, I'm a pretty good listener," Rachel offered.

"Yeah, you are. And you're pretty patient too, to have put up with my old ugly self for the past month. I know I've been a real jerk sometimes, and believe me, it has nothing to do with you. Well, no, that's not entirely true."

Finally turning toward Rachel, he said, "Look, why don't we get out and walk on the beach? We don't have to be at that party at any certain time, do we?"

"Of course not. In fact, it's just a come and go kind of thing. Some people aren't even coming until they finish the last shift in the dining room at the inn."

Leaving their shoes in the car, they strolled through the side yard of the unoccupied beach house in whose driveway they had parked, and when they reached the sand, Travis took off running. "Come on. I'll race you to the water. Last one there owes the other one a kiss," he yelled.

"Okay, you're on," Rachel called back. Smiling, she thought, *"Guess I never told you that I'm on the girl's track team at Miami. But then, I guess you never asked either, did you?"*

Standing by the water with her arms crossed and her lips puckered, Rachel couldn't help but giggle when a bewildered, winded Travis joined her seconds later. Dropping down on the sand, he managed a breathy "wow" before pulling Rachel down beside him. For the next few minutes, he said nothing; he just sat and threw empty periwinkle shells into the ocean.

"Well Rachel, it looks like you've won the right to an explanation," he finally relented. "I'm not sure exactly where to start; I guess my father's death would probably be as good a place as any. But I wish you would keep this to yourself for reasons that will become pretty obvious.

"See, there have been a lot of unanswered questions about the circumstances of Dad's accident...that is, until recently. Now, these Feds from Miami have come around saying that he was probably killed by some drug dealers who cut the brake lines on his truck. Apparently he stumbled onto them by mistake when he was hunting.

"It seems that the Narcs have been after these guys for some time, and the government now suspects that this bunch has been flying big loads in to the old Turner airfield. However, they haven't managed to intercept a load yet. They are questioning two guys - a drifter and some dude named Scotty who has a string of drug-related felonies. You probably read about that in the paper a few weeks ago. They've tried to down-play the story, because they're still trying to catch the rest of these guys. Anyway, it appears that there is a big, organized ring of them working in the area. Of course, with those F.B.I. guys driving around town in that mean black Volvo, wearing dead give-away suits - well, just how 'low-key' can you get? Anyway, here's where my problem comes in.

"Even though the family is still upset about Dad's senseless killing, we're at least relieved to finally have some sort of explanation and know that the Federal Authorities are working on the case. Mom, Trish and Aunt Emma are even trying to 'put it to rest' - and they should. Mom needs to get on with her life, and this should let her; so does Trish. But, Rachel, I don't think this thing is over, and the last thing I want to do is concern them any more, or, involve you, simply through association. I feel really frustrated because part of me wants to protect all of you from worrying, and part of me wants to scream at you to watch over your shoulder every second and not trust anybody! Then I get really mad because this is my hometown, and we've never had to worry about these kind of things.

"I just keep thinking 'Why can't those creeps crawl under a rock somewhere else and leave the good people around here alone?' I feel so angry and resentful, that sometimes I become almost obsessed with the hate. Logically, I know that these feelings are not good, and I shouldn't let them control me, but I can't seem to come to grips with them. It's like I want to find those guys myself and, well, I always seem to stop short of what I would do if I did find them. That in itself is frustrating. Hey, I'm a real prize, aren't I?"

Rachel stared out at the ocean through blurry eyes, and took a deep breath before speaking.

"Travis, you said something earlier about a penny for my thoughts. Well, nothing I might say would hold a candle to what you have just said to me. And, believe me, I realize how hard that must have been for you to be so painfully honest, especially with someone who you have only known for a short amount of time, but please know that you can trust me with this."

Rachel sighed and wrapped her arms around her knees.

"My real dad used to talk to me about everything, and he taught me to express my feelings openly," she continued. "After he died, Mom married Vince, and I sometimes wonder if an honest word has ever come out of his mouth. He's just so secretive about everything.

"I guess when you're in the business he's in, moving around a lot and saying what you think people want to hear becomes second nature. Oh, he's been an okay provider for Mom and me, but if I hadn't learned the importance of openness from my real dad, I might be as close-mouthed as Mom has become. So you see, I can identify with a lot more of your pain than you might have realized." Rachel turned to face Travis.

"Now, tell me more. Then, I expect you to give me enough credit to make my own decisions about any further involvement."

Travis grabbed a handful of white, powdery sand and let it dribble out slowly into a pile. He seemed to relax slightly as he faced Rachel.

"Yeah, okay, I guess that's only fair," Travis conceded. "Of course you're probably going to think I'm paranoid or something, but there is just an awful lot going on that can't be explained. For instance, what happened to us that night of our first date. You know it might not mean too much if that was just an isolated incident, but that same morning, some guys out on 98 found the remains of that body that washed up on the shore of an inlet. Looks like the dude was shot in the head. He had obviously been in the water for a while, but the timing still seems strange.

"Also, there have been seven other reported thefts on the island besides your parent's. And, speaking of problems on the island, Trish tells me that someone purposefully smashed several baby turtle nests this week.

"Some strange things have been going on in town, too. Like, we have been receiving some weird phone calls at our house. Sometimes they just sit and breathe heavily, and sometimes they kind of whisper in a raspy way. It's hard to tell what they are saying, and the weird thing is that they usually talk only when Aunt Emma answers, and she can't understand them. Then, just the other night, some of the guests at The Hopkins House Inn complained that someone had been looking in their window. I'm surprised that you didn't hear about that at work. The next day, they found that several of the guest's cars had been broken into, but when the police wanted to know what had been taken, one of the guys clammed up and said it wasn't important. Go figure.

"See, I keep thinking that if there is some kind of drug operation around here, and they have seen the Feds and think we know something about them, then we just might be in some kind of danger."

"Yeah, I see what you mean, Travis. And, no, I don't think it's crazy. In fact, I couldn't agree with you more. But why would big time drug dealers be doing strange things like looking in windows and smashing turtle eggs? Something doesn't quite add up. Oh well, it looks like I'm involved now anyway, like it or not, doesn't it? And it's okay; actually, it's a little bit exciting."

Rachel thought for a minute before continuing. "They say that two heads are usually better than one at solving a problem. So, let's work on this thing together - no more of that shutting me out stuff, okay?"

"Yeah, well if you're sure that's the way you want it." Travis said as he wrapped a gentle arm around her shoulders. "In fact," he continued with a slow grin, "why don't we start right now. Seems to me it takes two heads to manage a decent kiss, and I think I remember owing you one."

In the back of his mind, Travis was remembering another kiss, two months ago, when he had told Lorraine good-bye for the summer. She had already called once, from Maidstone, Kent in England where her family lived, to see if he would be able to come over in August. He had earlier entertained the idea of going, but considering the unexpected events of the summer, such a trip seemed unlikely.

Chapter 12

Choose a job that you love, and you will never have to work a day in your life.

Confucius

As summer progressed, so did the repairs from the tornado damage. The town appeared to take on a rather new, fresh, cosmopolitan look, with a hint of the international rather than the provincial. Remodeled storefronts displayed brightly colored doors, a bit of Irish influence, while the old cotton warehouses down by the river were revealing a touch of French charm, with additional balconies and courtyards.

In direct contrast to these improvements, many of the older buildings in town which had been left untouched by the tornado, stood proudly among the others with a quiet dignity and charm of their own. Most people considered the combined eclectic effect to be quite appealing.

Included among the older relics was a two-story, turn of the century frame building which housed the town's only printing shop and the offices of Apalachicola's newspaper. The only hint to the flurry of activity taking place behind the six-foot, double glass doors was a free-standing, wooden sign propped up against the front of the building beneath one of the unadorned, plate glass windows. In large, hand-painted, dark green letters, it simply said, THE VILLAGE VOICE.

The Owner and Managing Editor of the publication, Samuel Wilson Penton, was one of the town's most colorful assets. His casual, laid-back appearance was in direct contrast to his vigorous, flamboyant nature, and his sense of humor and adventure was experienced by most people as they walked through the front doors of the modest building.

Upon entering, one found it necessary to veer left in order to dodge the large stuffed boar waiting just inside the door. His discolored, mammoth fangs threatened to stab anyone curious enough to come near, and his eyes seemed to bore holes through even the most innocent. A loaded Polaroid camera sat on a desk across the room, and whenever a newcomer entered, they were invited to have their picture made next to the imposing creature.

Sam was a self-professed collector, his relics including not only displayable items such as guns, antiques and crafts, but the less tangible things such as personalities, legends, and human interest stories. Although he seldom acknowledged the fact, he was only too glad to share if it was for the betterment of his community or the delight of an interested party. And one of his favorite forms of sharing was verbal.

One of Sam's closest friends fondly liked to say that he had the Irish "gift of gab," combined with the Jewish sense of devotion, although he was neither by heritage. His own experiences, as well as those of friends, family, and even spot acquaintances, were the source of many intriguing tales. He had been known to captivate audiences of all size and age ranges, from large groups of Boy Scouts by the hundreds at Jamboree, to small groups of tourists out for an afternoon stroll.

Sam often said, with a twinkle in his grey eyes, "There's a story behind everything, and it's usually better with a little embellishment." It was little wonder that Emmaline Harris, former English / Drama Teacher, was one of his biggest fans. Not only was she enthralled with his animated recitations - "That boy would have received A's in my classes," she loved to say, but her background proved to be a fascinating source for some of Sam's many anecdotes. Together, they had a mutual admiration society.

One fine morning in July, the weather unusually pleasant after the insufferable heat of June, Sam decided to pay Emmaline Harris a visit. He suspected that he would find her out working in her herb garden, before the morning sun rose too high in the sky. He was looking forward to a nice chat with his friend, anxious to hear her most recent thoughts on the series of articles that he was writing about her herb garden.

His wife, Annie, had been after him, since reading the articles, to take her the next time he visited Mrs. Harris. Annie had recently become enamored with the 'natural' approach to life, determined to cure any ills and wrinkles by using home-grown plants and recipes, and she was interested in starting a garden of her own.

If she had not been in teacher workshops, he would have asked Annie to come along this morning. He regretted that they had been out of town when Libbie had invited them to supper club recently in her home.

Enjoying the casual stroll from his office to the Whitestone house, only three blocks away, he took in the sights and sounds of his town with a pride akin to that of a native parent. Sam was, admittedly, a transplant from Wyoming who remained true to his western upbringing, but made no apologies for his devotion to his present hometown.

Looking toward the Gorrie Bridge, named for the town's famous Dr. John Gorrie, who invented the first ice machine in 1850, Sam watched the last of the morning's refrigerated delivery trucks heading out of town to deliver the day's fresh catch to the nearby cities. Back at the docks, the riverfront cats scavenged for leftovers, carefully avoiding the diving gulls who considered all remaining seafood scraps to be theirs. The gulls' demanding squawks were in sharp contrast to the gentle coo of the pigeons who sat regally on telephone wires, watching the activity with a bored air of condescension.

Lawnmowers hummed busily around the court house, and the fresh smell of cut grass brought a smile of satisfaction to Sam's face. He gratefully thought how preferable it was to the sour odor which used to drift over on cloudy days from the nearby Port St. Joe Paper Mill.

Along the sidewalk, in the shadier areas, a few diehard crickets still serenaded with the last verses of the previous night's lovesongs, either not realizing that morning had come, or not caring. Adding his own tune to the symphony, Sam whistled a clear, melodious version of *The Sound of Music* theme song, Ms. Emma's favorite. There had been a time a year or so ago when she might have heard him coming.

A few blocks away, another whistler was headed in Sam's direction, carefully making his way along the sidewalk on a wobbly, blue bike. As he got nearer, his face broke into a wide grin.

"Mornin', Mr. Sam; where you headed?"

"Why, Jimmy Johns, how in the world are you, Preacher Man? I haven't seen you in a while. I'm headed over to visit Ms. Emmaline Harris and check on her garden. Care to join me?"

Balancing with one foot on the ground while he held onto the rickety bike, Jimmy answered. "Gee, I wished I could, Mr. Sam, but I'm on my way to th' hardware store to get me some tools to work on this here bike with. You know the church bought me a new bike after this one got all messed up in the tornado. So, I'm gonna fix this one up for my new frien'."

"Oh, who is that Jimmy?"

"Alls I know is his name's Rex. He lives aroun' out there near me and mom somewhere, and sometimes he catches a ride into town with me on the back of my new bike. So, I thought I might just fix up this here old bike for him."

"Well, that's very nice of you, Jimmy. And, I'm glad to hear that you have a new friend. I'd like to meet him sometime."

"Yes, sir, I'd sure like for you to. But, he don't like to be aroun' people much yet, 'cept for me, you see. I figure he's just kinda shy, but I'm workin' on him. You know, Ms. Libbie says I ain't never met a stranger," Jimmy said, with a confident grin.

"See ya, Mr. Sam," he said as he tipped his Atlanta Braves cap and rode off singing:

>"Amazin' grace, how sweet th' soun'
>that saved a wretch like me—"

Sam smiled and thought to himself, *"Jimmy, you're about the least wretched person I know. In fact, Libbie's right; your friendliness ought to be shared with more people. Maybe it's about time that I did a feature story on you in The Village Voice."*

As he approached the Whitestone home, he noticed a familiar black Volvo with a Dade County tag parked out front.

"Well, what do you know? Looks like the Feds are back. I wonder what's up?" he thought, as he quickened his steps.

Chapter 13

Our external environment is as important as our internal environment and, with good herbal influence, should bring balance and harmony.
Old Ming Dynasty philosophy

Pete's insistent barking announced Sam's arrival, and Libbie's face relaxed visibly when she opened the door.

"Oh Sam, I'm so glad you're here. Please, come in and have some coffee."

"Thanks, Lib, don't mind if I do; especially if the Miami Vice is here again bothering you."

"Well, yes, I mean, no, they aren't trying to. It's just that I thought we had most of this behind us, and it's naturally a little unsettling for them to come around again, especially unannounced. Really, I'm not sure why they are here this time. They didn't call; they just showed up early this morning."

Libbie grinned slightly. "Actually, they've been pretty nice. Aunt Emma invited them out back to see her herb garden the minute they got here. She was getting her bonnet out of the front closet, and when they came to the front door, she practically ushered them through the house, giving them a lesson on the importance of early morning cultivation. You know it's hard to tell her no, and they were surprisingly polite about going."

Sam followed Libbie into the kitchen.

"Good," he replied. "The last time they were here, I got the impression that they were a little stiff. Maybe Ms. Emma can help them lighten up some."

Libbie's bright, spacious kitchen / breakfast room was always inviting and cheerful with its blue gingham curtains, soft yellow walls, and wide heart pine floors, laid when the house had been built, and recently pickled to match the new cabinets. Years ago, Libbie and Rob had knocked out the end wall of the kitchen, opening it up to the adjoining parlor, which was now the breakfast room. Across the back wall of this room was the original brick fireplace with a lovely, old carved oak mantle. The adjoining side wall consisted of floor-to-ceiling windows that looked out on a wooden deck surrounded by azalea bushes and crape myrtle trees.

The antique, round oak table in the middle of the room displayed an arrangement of fresh flowers, thanks to Aunt Emma, and the matching sideboard was home to a huge, hand-painted, ceramic fish soup tureen. The walls were adorned with several of Libbie's original oil paintings, mostly florals and still-life pictures of fruit. Next to the fireplace sat Rob's blue leather chair and ottoman. Completing the picture, Repeat, the furry grey cat, could usually be found curled up on the colorful braided rug in front of the hearth.

The smell of freshly brewed coffee proved to be too tempting for Sam, who had promised Annie that he would cut back on his caffeine as well as his caloric intake.

"Just half a cup, Libbie. I've already had my limit this morning."

As he pulled out a ladder back chair to sit down at the breakfast table, a movement on the deck caught his eye. Aunt Emma was shuffling, faster than usual, toward the french doors, followed by two dark-haired gentlemen whose ties had been loosened, and suit coats removed, folded neatly over an arm.

"Oh dear me, dear me," Aunt Emma exclaimed as she hurried in the door, shaking her head. "Who would want to do such a thing? Oh, Libbie, it's such a mess, you won't believe it. My beautiful herb garden is trampled to pieces. It looks like someone stomped all through it on purpose, just trying to ruin it."

Lowering her bent little body into a chair, with help from Sam, Emmaline lovingly laid out on the table crumpled bits of rosemary and basil, two of her favorite herbs.

"Oh, Libbie, do you have time to help me snip and salvage what little I can save? We'll take the decent sprigs and tie them together to dry, but we'll need to chop up the culinary ones and freeze them in ice trays. I'm not too worried about the mint and the lemon balm. That stuff needed to be thinned out anyway. I told these nice young men here to pick all of the mint they want and enjoy it in their ice tea while they're in town. They're staying at the Hopkins' Inn, you know.

"Oh dear, I'm rambling, aren't I?" Addressing the two visitors from Miami who were politely standing just inside the door, she continued, "I'm so sorry, gentlemen, if I have appeared to be rude, but I'm just distraught. You see, vandalism has not been a problem around here, until recently, isn't that right, Sam, Libbie? But lately, well, I just don't know what to think. I feel completely violated."

The taller of the two men spoke first. "Yes ma'am, it appears that someone definitely **meant to** get your attention."

Emmaline immediately perked up. "**Men? Two**, did you say?" she asked, repeating what she mistakenly thought he had said. "Well, my goodness, I'm impressed. How did you already figure that out? You must have checked for footprints. Libbie, I think we're very lucky to have these gentlemen working on Rob's case. They seem to know what they're doing."

Sensing the men's confusion, Libbie expertly guided the conversation away from alleged footprints and vandals. She would find out later what that was all about.

"Emmie, I've already called the studio this morning and told them I won't be in. There are two other resident artists available who can run the place today, so I'll have plenty of time to help you. But right now why don't you help me serve our guests?"

Libby opened the oven door and, once again, Sam's resolve was tempted, this time by the tantalizing, fresh-baked aroma of cinnamon nut coffee cake.

"Gentlemen, I give you Aunt Emma's secret recipe 'Breakfast Buddy Delight', guaranteed to make you her friend for life," Libbie announced, pleased to see her aunt beaming triumphantly.

"*Sorry, Annie,*" Sam thought. "*I can't pass this up and risk hurting Ms. Emmaline Harris' feelings.*" he rationalized, as he helped himself to more coffee.

* * *

"*Dang, Mrs. Harris, I'm sorry. I didn't mean to get you all upset like that. I just wanted to get you out in your garden for a while, so I could talk to you. I really didn't mean to tear it all up; Looks like I lost control again.*

"*Crud! I wish I wouldn't get so mad like that, but seeing this nice house and those bad cars that the kids drive, and everything so clean and perfect, it just makes me feel like I want to hate somebody or something. Sometimes I even want to hurt somebody ....That scares me, Mrs. Harris 'cause it seems like I'm more like my old man than I ever wanted to be.*

"*Well, it don't seem fair anyway when I think about the way I grew up. Heck, somebody was always hurtin' me, weren't they? Yeah, I still remember hidin' under my bed listenin' to my mom's screams. I wanted to help her - she was about the only person who was good to me, but I knew he'd kill me if he got half a chance. He was always so mean and hateful when he came around, and she was always so scared, but she would never leave. She just kept on letting it happen.*

About the only smart thing I ever did was to get out of that situation. And then it backfired on me. Mrs. Harris, that's one of the reasons I really wanted to talk to you. No one else would ever listen to me, but I was hoping maybe you would. Now I've probably screwed up my chances for good! I guess I should have told you on the phone, but everytime I've called, it sounded like someone else was listening in and I would chicken out....yeah, the story of my life."

Chapter 14

*Man's mind, once stretched by a new idea,
never regains its original dimension.*
                              Oliver Wendell Holmes

Pete's sudden barking once again announced the arrival of unexpected company. Emmaline adjusted her hearing aid and turned to Libbie.

"Was that the bell, Dearie? My goodness, we must have more visitors."

"Yes, Emmie, that was the doorbell." Libbie answered. "I imagine that Trish will answer it. I heard her come downstairs a few minutes ago."

"Good morning, everyone." Matt said as he followed Trish into the bright kitchen. "Am I interrupting something?"

"No, of course not, Matt," Libbie assured him. "You're just in time for some of Aunt Emma's coffee cake."

"Boy, is my timing ever right," Matt grinned. "Thanks, Lib. I believe I will have a piece. It smells too good to pass up. Sam, how are you? Gentlemen, I'm Matthew Douglas," he said, offering his hand to first one and then the other of the strangers in the kitchen.

The second of the Miami duo finally spoke. "Nice to meet you, sir. I'm Roland Harper from the Federal Bureau of Investigation, and this is my partner, Emerson Vaughn."

Matt poured himself a cup of coffee, accepted the cake from Libbie, and settled comfortably into Rob's leather chair.

"Hmm, he seems right at home," Sam thought, his natural instincts for a story kicking in. *"I wonder—"*

Out loud he said, "Matt, what brings you out so early on a Monday morning?"

"Funny you should ask, Sam. As a matter of fact, after I visited Libbie and Ms. Emma, I was coming to see you today. It seems that I have been asked to take over as the back-up chairman of the Seafood Festival in November. But then, you already knew that didn't you?" Matt said, winking at Libbie. "In fact, Sam, someone told me that you were one of my biggest supporters when Mavis nominated me to take Mr. Stokes' place. Incidentally, that's too bad about his back surgery, but I hear that he's recovering nicely.

"Actually, I don't mind taking over for him; I'm glad to be able do my part this year, especially with all of the support that I know that I can expect from good folks like you, Sam, right? Of course, Ms. Emma has already promised to make herbal teas and jellies for concessions," he continued, completely unaware of the morning's trauma. "And Libbie has offered one of her paintings to be raffled off. I guess it's all right to tell that it's her painting of the sunset - the picture that won first place in the Big Bend Art Contest." He glanced at Libbie who nodded her approval.

"By the way, this is probably as good a time as any to start soliciting. You see, I have had an idea for a new fund raiser, and, even though it's kind of late in the game, I think we might have time to pull this thing off. I'll go into more detail later, but let me run the basic idea by all of you and see what you think.

"It has occurred to me, throughout the past year that I have been blessed to live here, that we have an abundance of local talent. The one that most often intrigues me is the story-telling that goes on, and I do consider the ability to 'spin a yarn,' as my grandmother used to say, to be a real gift.

"So, what do you all think about having a 'Biggest Mouth in Town' contest, with the contestants raising money over the next few months from their supporters who buy voting slips in support of their favorite candidate? Sam, I already know that between you and Jimbo Hopkins, we could raise a lot of money. Of course, you know I mean that as a compliment, don't you?" Encouraged by the enthusiasm that he saw reflected in their faces, Matt continued.

"We could have large, painted fish faces around town with their mouths open for people to drop vote ballots into, and the local businesses could sell the ballots. People could buy as many ballots as they wish for, say $1.00 a piece. Then, on Friday night of the festival, the contestants could have a run-off, with each telling their favorite tale. People in the crowd could vote one more time that night with ballots which would be sold there in the park.

"They do something similar to this in Dallas to raise money for cancer, and it is always a tremendous success. I'm sure that there is a worthwhile project around here that could benefit from the proceeds."

Matt paused to take a sip of his coffee and a bite of Ms. Emma's cake before continuing. A glance at the men from Miami revealed a look of impatience on their normally stoic faces, and Roland, seizing the moment, quickly spoke up.

"I beg your pardon sir, but if you will excuse us, we need to speak with Mrs. Whitestone privately." Without waiting for an answer, he turned to Libbie and asked, "Is there another room where we might go?"

Libbie's reserve momentarily appeared to falter, before she regained control and graciously invited them into the den. Sam and Matt frowned, slightly offended by the men's abrupt exit. However, their strongest concern was for Libbie, each wanting to protect her from the mental anguish that these two strangers might induce. As they started to rise and follow the trio, Emmaline Harris put up her hand, and with her authoritative teacher voice and a wisdom that defied most obstacles, she characteristically took control.

"Trish, dear, you go on in there with your mom, but try to let her handle this by herself as much as possible." she instructed. "You just be there for her if she needs you."

Turning to Matt and Sam she said, "Now you two gentlemen have a seat. Libbie will be all right. She's still taking baby steps, but I see signs of her running at full speed very soon. By the way," Emmaline remarked, skillfully changing the subject, "have I ever told you guys about her first tricycle? No, I'm sure I haven't.

"Well, you see, her mom and dad had hidden it in the hall closet the week before Christmas. But, Miss Libbie was looking for her kitty one day - or was it her puppy? Oh well, that's not important. Anyway, she found the tricycle and proceeded to take it out and ride it, apparently quite well, until she got it stuck on the floor heater. When she tried to climb off, she fell, and the backs of her little legs looked like a waffle iron had branded her.

"Now I don't need to tell you that she was scared to death of that floor heater for quite a while. Her dad kept saying, 'Leave her alone and let her work through it on her own. She'll be okay.'

"Sure enough, they started hearing that little three year old in the mornings singing 'Jesus Loves Me' after breakfast, while she slowly circled that hot floor vent. One day, her mom heard her yell 'AND HE IS STRONG!' She rushed to the hall door to see little miss Elizabeth jumping up and down on the vent, clapping and laughing. 'Look Mommie,' she called. 'Jesus is so strong he picks me up, and this old heater can't hurt me anymore.'

"Gentlemen, to this day she has had that unrelenting faith. I'm not worried about her, no sirree."

Matt felt a humbling sense of gratitude to this precious little lady for the dose of faith that she had so delightfully shared. Maybe he ought to ask her if she wanted to enter the story-telling contest.

Sam was intrigued also. However, for once, this was not a story he relished for its repeatable value. Rather, he, who unquestionably acknowledged the presence of a Supreme Being but was not much of a church goer, tucked it away to ponder later, probably in the wee small hours of the night when he did his best thinking.

Supper at the Whitestone's house that night was a rather somber affair. Earlier in the day, when Travis had come home for lunch, he had found two visibly upset ladies. His Aunt Emma had been hard at work preparing ice trays of herb bits for freezing, while indulging in one of her more blasphemous expressions, reserved for her most traumatic moments.

"Hell's bells and cow's aunts," she had clucked over and over, shaking her head all the while.

Years ago Emmaline Harris had warned the family that the only cussing she would tolerate would be her own. No one had ever challenged her, and so far her questionable attempts at profanity had been more amusing than serious.

Libbie had been helping his aunt separate and cup up the herbs, and the normally organized kitchen was a disaster.

"Oh, Travis honey," Libbie had said. "I'm afraid that I haven't had time to fix you any lunch. Someone tore Aunt Emma's garden all to pieces last night, and we've been trying to salvage what we can this morning. Also, those F.B.I. men were here again, and they, along with Sheriff Coggins, had Trish and me looking through countless pictures of suspects. They have just left, and Trish has finally gone on to work, but lunch has been the farthest thing from my mind."

Neither Libbie nor Trish had been able to positively recognize or identify anyone in the pictures, but Trish had an uncomfortable feeling about one of them...something about the man's eyes. She had not said anything to the agents, but she did mention it to the family that night at the dinner table.

"Come on honey; don't let those guys spook you," Libbie urged. "You probably just got caught up in the power of suggestion."

"No, Mom...the more I think about it, the more those eyes haunt me! They had a kind of yearning but, at the same time, a shiftless, sinister look, like they wanted to look at you longer, but couldn't risk it. I have had that same feeling a time or two this summer, when I felt like this guy was watching me, but he would turn away quickly when I looked."

"Aw Trish," Travis exclaimed. "Why haven't you told me about this before now? I might as well tell all of you that I haven't felt good about any of this drug ring business, especially with all of those phone calls, robberies and stuff - and now, Aunt Emma's garden. The weird thing is how it all just started happening this summer since Trish and I have been home from school."

"Well, that's not exactly true, Travis," Libbie said. "The robberies actually started back shortly after Valentine's day. Emmie, do you remember that George had given Fran that beautiful watch for a valentine present? Well, that same week her purse was stolen from her car, and the watch was in it. She was on her way to Panama City for the day and was going to have the watch band sized while she was over there. Ralph and Paula had supper club the next night, and that was the main topic of conversation."

"Yeah, and anyway, Travis," Trish chimed in. "Why would big-time drug dealers be stealing purses and breaking into houses? Even more, I don't think they would be spending much time stomping through herb gardens, peeping in windows and making crazy phone calls."

"I know, Trish; I agree with you. But facts are facts, and there have been two unsolved deaths in the past year and a half, one of them being our own father's. Some of this stuff at least has to be related to that. Hey look, I'm worried about all of you. I want the three of you to promise me that you will be extra careful from now on until this thing is settled. Keep the doors locked when you're home alone, lock your car doors, and none of you need to be going out at night without a male - preferably me, Wes or Matt.

"Also, I'm going to buy one of those caller-ID boxes tomorrow, so maybe we can find out where this pervert is calling from. By the way, did either of you mention those calls to the F.B.I. guys?"

"No, I didn't," Libbie said. "Did you, Trish?"

"No, I didn't think it was important to them. All they seemed interested in were those weird pictures. I hate the thought of looking through them again tomorrow."

"They're coming back tomorrow?" Travis asked. "Well, I'll just have to be a little bit late to work. I'm sure Buddy will understand when I tell him why."

"Did you say those men are coming again tomorrow?" Aunt Emma asked, pleased that she had been able to follow most of the dinner conversation. "Well, I certainly want to have a look at those pictures, myself, this time. And," she added, "I think that I will order some more of those hanging door alarms. Maybe they have improved them so that one can hear them now."

Chapter 15

This was one of those rye-bread days - all dull and damp without.

Margaret Fuller

Tuesday morning was dreary and stormy, reminiscent of the nasty morning back in May that had spawned the tornado. Street lights were still on at 8:00 A.M., confused by the dark, turbulent sky.

Jimmy Johns snapped on his yellow, patrol boy raincoat and tightened the hood over his Pittsburgh Steelers cap, a gift from Harold and Sarah Greenberg. Outside, the wind roared as it whipped around the corners, rattling the windows and doors of the little house trailer that Jimmy and his mom called home. Jimmy steadied himself against the walls of the narrow hall as the whole trailer shook.

"Ma," he called. "I've got to go to work now. Are ya' gonna be okay? You was coughin' mighty bad last night."

Propped up in bed, Virginia Johns (Ginger to her few friends) took a long, last puff of her cigarette and dropped the stub into her coffee cup.

"You go on to work now, boy. This ain't nuthin' but a little summer cold. And quit worryin' about me, you hear? I'll be just fine. You know I love ya boy, and I'm mighty proud of you too."

"Yes'm, I reckon I do know it by now. I'll see ya this evenin'. I might be a little late, 'cause I'm gonna try to meet up with my new buddy and give him my old bike. You need anything, Ma?"

"No, boy, not unless some of your customers is givin' out some good looks today."

"Hey, that's a good one, ma. You must be feelin' better. See ya."

* * *

A loud clap of thunder jolted the man awake to the fuzzy realization that rain was dripping on his face, and something slimy was crawling across his foot. He jerked up quickly, too quickly for his ravaged body, and immediately he rolled back down onto the hard, dirty floor, clutching his head to keep it from splitting apart.

"Oh crud! Man, what was in that joint last night? Those lousy creeps, claimin' to be Scotty's buddies. Yeah, some friends. They

should have given me top quality for all that jewelry I had. Whatever those dregs were, I feel like warmed-over death this morning, or is it afternoon?

"I can't even remember how much money they paid me, or how I got here, wherever 'here' is."

Reaching into his pocket, he soon realized that there was, in fact, no money. His old vinyl billfold lay empty on the floor next to him. Not only had they not paid him for the jewelry, but they had also taken what little cash he had on him.

"Those freaks rolled me, too! Nah, this ain't happenin'. Ooh, I feel like a Mack truck ran over me. My eyes are so blurry. Maybe I need to sleep a little longer; make this headache go away. Man, my mouth's dry!"

By 10:00, the torrential downpour had subsided to a steady drizzle, with no sign of letting up.

"It's just as well that those guys are coming this morning," Travis commented to Trish as they looked out the window at the soggy remains of their aunt's little garden. "You can't go looking for baby turtles in this mess, and for sure, me and Wes can't be putting a roof on Matt's island house. Besides, I'm curious to see the pictures that they are bringing over. Hey Trish, be sure to point out the one that concerned you this time."

At exactly 10:30, the punctual agents showed up. Travis led them into the den with a chilled politeness. He wasn't sure why they irritated him so much. Maybe it was their painful reminder of his father's unfortunate death, maybe it was their manicured smirk; probably it was both.

"Good morning, gentlemen. Would you like coffee?" Emmaline Harris offered, ever the perfect hostess.

"No thank you, ma'am. We've got to go into Tallahassee today, and we don't want to take up any more of your time than necessary," Roland answered, as he laid large books on the coffee table.

"We brought some extra pictures today. If you don't mind, we'd like for all of you to look through them this time, and if one of the faces looks even slightly familiar, write the person's name down. If you find anyone, we'll compare the names when you're through for similarities."

The four spent the next hour combing through the pictures, occasionally jotting down a name. Near the end of the third book, Emmaline exclaimed, "Well my goodness, if that doesn't look like J.R. - Junior, we always called him. Oh dear, what was his name? He was one of my students the last year that I taught. He was a very intelligent young man, but he never performed up to his ability; he always seemed to be worried about something. It seems like I did hear about him being in some kind of trouble after I retired.

"This couldn't be him, though. This says Robert Sloan under the picture. Anyway, he had lighter hair as I remember."

"Mrs. Harris, this man is wanted for suspicion of murder - his own mother, as a matter of fact. He's considered to be extremely dangerous," Lowell said. "Do you think there's any possibility that this is the same man?"

"Let me see, Aunt Emma," Trish called, coming over to her aunt's rocker.

"Oh my gosh," she cried, staring into the somber-looking face of a slightly overweight young man with long, greasy dark hair tucked behind his ears and hanging to his shoulders. The shifty brown eyes seemed to bore a hole right through her.

"That's him. That's the guy that I was suspicious of in the picture yesterday. I'm sure, now that I see those eyes again. I know that I've seen him around several times this summer, although his face isn't that pudgy anymore. And look at his possible alias names - John or Robert."

"That's it," Emmaline chimed in. "John Robert was his name. He always signed his papers J.R. I don't remember Sloan being his last name, but then, I can't seem to remember what his last name was anyway. Please, may I see that picture again?"

At lunchtime, Jimmy Johns rode around looking for his new friend. Jimmy was never quite sure where his buddy would be; he usually seemed to pop up out of nowhere.

The rain had finally stopped, and the steam rising from the street and sidewalks gave testimony to the abundance of leftover heat and humidity. Jimmy folded his raincoat and stuffed it into his bike bag, making sure to leave enough room for his afternoon newspapers.

"Hey, Preacher Man, what's up?" Wes called as he climbed out of his truck in front of Trish's house.

Jimmy waved and crossed the street to visit with one of his favorite people. "Hey, Mr. Seminole. Too bad I didn't run into you yesterday; I was wearin' my Florida State cap that you give me."

"Good for you, Jimmy. You need to wear it a lot when football season starts."

"I sure will, 'specially ever time I watch ya on the TV. You know y'all are my fav'rit team. Course Mr. Jimbo now, he gives me a hard time if I don't wear th' gator cap he give me too. Hey, when do ya hafta leave to start your football practice?"

"Ow," Wes grimaced. "Don't remind me, man; it's too soon. Coach wants us back August 12. At least Trish doesn't have to go back to Auburn until the middle of September, so we can see each other on the weekends off and on until then."

Jimmy smiled his snaggled-tooth grin and said, "I've been recognizin' you two was doin' some serious courtin around here. Miss Trish, she sure is purty, an' she's mighty nice too."

Wes gave Jimmy a friendly pat on the back, saying, "Yeah, she sure is, Jimmy. In fact, I was just about to go in and see her. Come on, I know they'd like to see you too."

"I don't know," Jimmy said. "I'm on my lunch hour, and it looks like they've got a bunch of comp'ny anyways. Wonder why Sheriff Coggin is there?"

"I'm not sure, Jimmy. Trish called me and said something about coming over to see some F.B.I. pictures. Maybe ol' Bernie Cog is looking at them too.

Across the street, Travis came out on the front porch and yelled, "Hey Wes, Jimmy; you guys come on over here. We've got something for you to look at."

When they entered the Whitestone den, Jimmy drew back slightly, a little confused by the commotion. All three women were talking excitedly, and all at the same time. They were acting more like the ladies in his mom's soap operas than the normally reserved Libbie, Trish and Ms. Emma that he was used to.

"Wes, what took you so long? This is really important," Trish fussed. "Oh, hey Jimmy, good to see you," she said in a softer voice.

"Why, Jimmy Johns," Aunt Emma said. "What brings you out this early on such a dreary day? I wasn't expecting to see you until you delivered the paper this afternoon, but it certainly is nice to have you drop by. You should do so more often."

"Jimmy, how are you?" Libbie joined in. "How's your mother?"

Basking in the glow of so much attention, Jimmy relaxed and answered enthusiastically, "She's doin' all right, except for that pain and cripplin' in her back and legs; it just don't seem to go away. And she's had a pretty nasty cough the last coupla days."

"Jimmy, I have just the thing for that cough," Aunt Emma said as she carefully rose out of her rocker and shuffled toward the kitchen. "I'm going to give you some herbal tea bags that contain Ma Huang, peppermint, licorice and eucalyptus, plus a little ginger root and fennel seed. You tell her to drink a few warm cups of this tea each day and take the echinacea capsules that I'm going to give you to build up her immune system. Let me know next week how she's feeling. I wish I knew what to do for her legs. Maybe she can get some help when the new Rehabilitation Center opens."

"Gee thanks, Ms. Emma. But you know, we ain't got much money to be spendin' at hospitals and all. We do like to pay what we owe, but she can't pay nuthin' for them pills 'till her check comes in at th' end of th' month."

"Why fiddledy dee, Jimmy. I don't sell my herbs; I share them with my friends. Speaking of which," she turned at the kitchen door and directed her next comment to Roland, "young man, you could use some of my tea for that cough of yours, also."

Roland was tempted to tell her that his was a smoker's cough that got worse when he was under stress, and these lovely, laid-back, home-grown people were about to drive him crazy. What usually took a couple of hours from start to finish had already taken a couple of days in this relaxed, little town. The scary thing was that Emerson seemed to be enjoying it.

Instead he said, "Thank you ma'am. I believe I'll pass, since Emerson and I have so much to do and so little time." He stressed the last two words.

Emmaline Harris muttered something about the world passing him by without him ever so much as smelling a rose, and she continued into the kitchen.

Turning to Wes and Jimmy, Roland explained about the pictures and asked if they would mind looking through the books.

"I ain't sure I understand who we're lookin' for," Jimmy said, becoming a little uneasy with this man's formality.

"Son, if you see anyone who looks at all familiar, just point them out. That's all these guys want you to do," Sheriff Coggins explained, noting Jimmy's discomfort.

Jimmy and Wes combed through the large books rather quickly, Jimmy worried about staying away too long for lunch - although he was sure Rev. Anderson would understand if it was official sheriffin business. Finally Wes said, "I may have seen this guy a time or two."

Looking over his shoulder, Trish broke into a wide grin and hugged him. "That's the one, Wes. That's who I've seen too, and guess what. Aunt Emma thinks she used to teach him in Panama City. Hey Jimmy," she continued, "Have you seen this book?"

"Yeah, but I didn't recognize nobody but maybe one girl in it."

"Come look again," Trish urged, closing the book so that the picture Wes had identified wouldn't be obvious to Jimmy. Roland had instructed them not to reveal any previously recognized pictures, so that there would be no chance of influence through suggestion.

Jimmy opened the book and carefully looked back through, finally stopping on a page. "Here she is. This here girl is th' only person in this book that I might of seen. She looks kinda like that girl I see sometimes at th' Stop 'n Shop, 'cept her hair is diff'rent. I've looked real closelike at her before 'cause she's got this funny little hole in her chin, just like this here girl. When she smiles, it kinda goes away, but she don't smile too much."

Bernie Coggins read the name under the picture and asked if anyone had ever heard of Barbara Bellinger. The name wasn't familiar to anyone, but they all rushed over to look. Only Aunt Emma thought that she might have seen the girl before, but she couldn't begin to place where - or even if - she had for sure.

Chapter 16

Awakened, he descends the far side of the dream.
Victor Hugo

"Psst! Hey you, wake up!"

The raspy whisper was an irritating intrusion, invading the very depths of his body and soul.

"Ignore it; it'll go away. It's just my stupid head playing tricks on me again."

"Come on you creep. I ain't got time to sit out here nursing you all night. I got to be at work in an hour. Now sit up and eat this soup I brought you. I want to make sure you ain't dead or nothing."

A small but surprisingly strong foot in a soft tennis shoe convincingly nudged at his ribs. Slowly rolling over on his side, he managed to prop up on his right arm and partially focus his eyes on a pair of shapely legs in black mesh hose.

"Great. I musta already died and gone to heaven. Mrs. Harris always said that God loved me," he mumbled, rubbing his hands through his greasy hair as he sat up and leaned against a wall.

"Hush up, you ungrateful slob, and listen to me. Now, I feel real bad, you see, about introducing you to them guys last night. I shoulda known better, but you was insistent, and I can't be taking time at work to get too involved, you know."

"Woman, you oughta feel bad. Whatever that rot gut was coulda killed me - and I don't even mess with the hard stuff. The last thing I remember was a whackin noise on my head, then a few stars. Let me tell you about feelin bad."

"Shh; keep your voice down and just let me finish, will you?" Bubbles said quietly. He just moaned and put his head in his hands.

Bubbles pulled an empty crate over from the nearest corner and dusted it off with a napkin that she took out of the bag of food in her hand. Sitting on one end of the crate, she spread a second napkin over the other end. Out of the bag she brought a styrofoam bowl which produced a steamy smell of chicken broth when she took the top off. Next came a jar of what appeared to be tea with ice cubes in it, followed by packs of saltine crackers. His queasy stomach wanted to be repulsed by the tempting aroma, but his somewhat diminished common sense knew better than to turn it down.

"Now, the way I see it, Ray, - or Jay - or whatever your name is, those guys are bad news. I ain't seen them around but a few other times, and they was always with your pal, Scotty. So when you wanted to find some of his friends last night, I figured you knew what you was doing." Bubbles opened the jar and passed it to him.

"You drink this tea real slow, you hear me, 'cause your stomach ain't going to hold much right off.

"Anyway, when I came out back to empty the garbage last night around 2:00, right after we closed, I seen those two running away from this shed. I wouldn't have thought too much about it, but I heard a groan right when I started to go back in. So, like an idiot, I figure I'll just have a look around, and that's when I seen you all sprawled out across the floor here; like to scared me to death. So, anyway, I checked to see if you was dead or not, and I took off. I sure was praying hard that you would make it until I got back here today, 'cause, like I said, I felt kind of responsible. I mean, you ain't been anything but real nice when you been in the place before, and I sure hated to see you leave with guys like that. By the way, what did you tell me your name was?"

Unable to remember which alias he might have used, he stalled for time while he reached for the soup and sipped a spoonful.

"I don't remember that I ever told you, but I know your name is Bubbles, so thank you, Bubbles, for the food. Aren't you taking a mighty big chance helping me like this when you don't even know my name?"

Bubbles pointedly looked at her watch as she stood up and slowly backed away.

"You're probably right Ray - or Jay. I don't know who you are, or what you're up to, but I do know that you seem like a pretty nice guy who's running from something or somebody. When I was growing up in Birmingham, I had a sweet little Jewish neighbor who used to tell me to be thankful for my blessings, and when I saw someone who was down on their luck, to share some of what I had with them. Well, the way I seen it, you was pretty down last night, and you don't look a whole lot better today. She also taught me how to make this matzo-ball chicken soup that you're slurping down over there; said that it'll cure most anything."

"Woman, you talk more than anybody I ever seen," he said as he tore open a pack of crackers, quickly adding, "Whoa, now. Don't go getting all huffy on me like that. Just be quiet for a minute, and let me get enough of this stuff in me to clear my head, OK?"

Bubbles crossed her arms and allowed herself a momentary pout before she spoke again. What was it about this man that interested her so? It certainly wasn't his grooming habits. Right now he looked and smelled like something that had just crawled out of a gutter.

It had to be his eyes. At times they looked almost gentle - friendly sort of, but at other times Bubbles detected a deep sense of sadness when she looked into them - which wasn't often. He generally tended to avoid direct eye contact.

"Well, excuse me please. But you don't have to listen to me no more, 'cause I've got my job to do," she said, trying to sound more perturbed than she really was.

"You can just throw those containers away in our dumpster behind the lounge, but don't let nobody see you. And you better get yourself on out of here soon. Old Jack don't come out here often, but you never know when he might decide to store some more junk in this old place."

"Hey, Bubbles," he called. "You coming back?"

"Have you been listening to me or not? I told you, my shift starts in five minutes, and I've got to go change into my waitress outfit. And you best not be coming in the place tonight, unless you get yourself cleaned up real good, you hear me? The Top Flite ain't the classiest place in town, but it ain't crawling neither. Now good evening to you."

He managed to stand up shakily and said, "Will you wait just a minute? How late do you work tonight?"

"I get off at 11:00 – short shift in the middle of the week. Why?"

"Well, if I get myself cleaned up, would you meet me back here when you leave? I don't guess I've properly thanked you and all."

"Now, why would I meet you out here at this old dirty storage shed? I'll be leaving out the front door like a lady ought to, and if I just happen to run into you, well, we'll see."

He managed a small chuckle, something that he had not done in some time.

"It's a date, Bubbles. And by the way, you can call me Jay."

He finished the food and was surprised that he was still hungry. Even more surprising was the fact that he actually felt somewhat better. After a good shower, he ought to feel almost good as new. The only problem was where to take one. He had promised Bubbles that he would get cleaned up, but he was miles from the outside shower at the old bay house where he had been hanging out, and he only had a few hours. His few pieces of clothing were there too, in the old cabin boat where he had been sleeping behind the house. This was going to call for some of that real thinking - that ingenuity stuff that Mrs. Harris used to say that he had if he would just use it.

Chapter 17

Do not conform any longer to the pattern of this world, but be ye transformed by the renewing of your mind.

Romans 12:2

At exactly 11:15, Bubbles exited the heavy, wooden front door of The Top Flite Lounge and Grill, bidding the muscular bouncer a good night. She fumbled in her purse for her keys, trying not to appear anxious by looking around too much. She stepped off of the porch and started out into the parking lot toward her car after a quick glance revealed no one nearby.

Employees were told to park out under the trees by the street in order to leave the closer spaces for customers, a policy which disgruntled the waitresses who had already been on their feet for hours. However, this evening was especially nice with a cool breeze blowing, and the clear sky full of stars. Bubbles was enjoying the walk for a change.

"You're late," a deep voice called out from between two cars. Seconds later, Jay strolled out and fell into step next to the petite blonde who had barely broken stride.

"Well, I don't recollect you being at the front door, yourself," Bubbles said, looking straight ahead. They walked the next few steps in silence until they reached her car. Finally turning to look at him, she smiled; "I will say that you look a little better."

"Just a little? Woman, I worked hard to look this good! And that's all you can say? I've even got a new shirt on for you."

"Yeah? I like it. The color matches your eyes. Where did you get it?"

"You don't want to know," he said, changing the conversation. "Come on, let's talk about where we go from here."

"I don't know about you," Bubbles responded, "but I was planning on going home to change clothes before I went to the camp meeting down the highway. You're welcome to come if you want to; might do you some good."

"Nah, I'm not much of one for meetings. I don't like to be around too many people. What's a camp meeting, anyway?"

"Well, it's like a church kind of revival that these preachers have in a big tent that they set up in an open field. It goes on for hours, and people come and go when they want to. It works for me, 'cause I can go when I get off from work at night. I mostly like to go to hear the music. They usually have some pretty good bands and people playing guitars, and they always play the old church songs that I learned when I was a little girl. It makes me feel real good to just sit on my blanket back in the field, away from the crowds, and sing along. Do you like to sing?"

"I don't know, Bubbles. I ain't sung in so long, I don't even know all the words to a whole song anymore. I used to listen to some country music 'cause my mama always had it on the radio."

"Yeah? Hop in and ride with me to the house. Maybe you'll change your mind."

Against his better judgment, Jay climbed in the little two door Honda, immediately moving the passenger seat back to accommodate his long legs. He knew better than to trust anybody, and he would have to be real careful not to get too involved with this cute little lady. She could be his ticket to big-time trouble.

"Trouble; that's a joke. Who am I fooling?" he thought. *"I'm already in so much trouble I don't know whether to sink or swim. But this is the first time in a while that I have halfway enjoyed myself. Heck, she's even made me smile a time or two. Surely I deserve a little fun. Life can't be all bad all the time."*

"Whoa, girl; who's been riding in this seat with such short legs?" he asked.

"That's where my little boy, Jody, sits. He's only five years old, and he's the love of my life. He'll probably be asleep when we get to the house, but you can meet him some other time if you want to."

"You married or something?" he asked, looking at the speedometer and wondering how fast she might go when she finally shifted into fifth, since she was going 70 now. "And, by the way, you ought not to speed along in fourth gear like that," he continued. "They put a fifth gear in these cars for cruising, you know, 'cept I don't think you better go much faster even in fifth. Seems to me there was a speed limit sign back there that said 50 miles per hour."

"What's th' matter? You scared or something?" Bubbles retorted. "Surely a rough, tough guy like yourself ain't worried about a little speed, are you? Maybe you're scared the cops might pull us over. Is that it, Jay? You think they might recognize you?"

"You didn't answer my question, woman. I don't hang with married women, so you might ought to let me out now, if that's the case."

Bubbles just smiled and slowed down, putting on her left blinker before turning into the driveway of a modest, pink concrete block house with a flat gravel roof. A quick survey of the overgrown front yard with a faded, wooden windmill standing knee deep in grass suggested to Jay that there was no man around, at least not one who did the yard work.

"You sure are good at changing the subject when you don't want to talk about something," Bubbles said, turning to face him in the crowded front seat. "And no, there's no old man – just me and Jodie and my sister.

"Now look, what's your business is your business," she continued. "That's okay with me, as long as it don't get me into trouble, or threaten me and my young'n. But, listen to me real good. If you're in some kind of big trouble with the law, man, I'm not your ticket, and I need to know it now. The least you can do is be honest enough with me to ease my mind. I don't think that's asking too much, do you?"

"Hey, gimme a break, woman," he thought with a frown. *"If I tell you the truth, you probably won't believe me either. And part of the truth is that I am wanted by the cops. Well, you said I was good at changing the subject. Maybe I can stall just a little longer, long enough to enjoy your company for the evening. Who knows? You just might decide that I'm OK.*

"Hey God, if you're really out there like Mrs. Harris always said you were, prove it to me. Yeah, let me enjoy tonight like a normal person," he challenged, wondering why he had even bothered.

Picking his words carefully, he answered her in his most sincere tone. "Look, I'm a real complicated person, and you're a real smart lady. Why don't you run on in and change while I wait out here for you. I don't want to make you uncomfortable around your kid and all. And I'll even go to that tent thing with you if we can sit back away from all the people. Maybe we can talk about some things then. You know I might just have a few questions for you too, like what is YOUR real name? And are you called Bubbles because of that cute dimple in your chin?"

Somewhat appeased, but less than satisfied, Bubbles smiled.

"Sounds good to me, Jay. I'll just be a minute. Why don't you go on around back and wait for me on the patio. We can walk down to the meeting. It's right across that field behind my house. You can probably hear them singing while you're waiting for me," she said.

As he carefully made his way through the tall grass around to the back yard, Jay did, indeed, hear music drifting across the open field. He sat down on a rickety lounge chair which was missing some plastic strips and smelled like suntan lotion. The evening breeze blew his long hair away from his face, and a lightning bug brazenly winked at him, right in front of his nose. The tops of several tall pine trees swayed in the breeze, as if dancing to the beat of the song which was now clear enough for him to make out some of the words:

> "I saw the light, Lord, I saw the light,
> no more sorrow, no more fright,
> Now I am happy ...."

"Jay, are you out there? I'm ready, but I need you to help me with this cooler. I figured you would probably be hungry again." Bubbles came out on the patio with her arms full. As Jay jumped up to help her, the contentment that he had felt the last few minutes strangely took the form of another almost prayerful thought:

"Hey, God, whoever you are, I wish you really were out here for me."

Chapter 18

We don't know one-millionth of one percent about anything!

Thomas Edison

"Mornin' Aunt Emma," Travis called as he stumbled sleepily into the kitchen with Pete following closely at his heels. "Where's Mom?"

"Well good morning yourself, young man. Aren't you up bright and early for a Saturday morning?" Emmaline answered as she popped another piece of bread into the toaster. "I hope that you will join me for some of my homemade fig preserves on toast. These are the preserves that I plan to sell at the Seafood Festival, and I need an objective opinion. I'm afraid that they are a little too sweet."

"Your mother just left with Trish for the grocery store. I hear that the girls are cooking some kind of fancy dinner for you and Wes tonight."

"Yes ma'am, that's what they tell me. You know that Wes has to report back to school on Monday for football."

Travis poured a large glass of milk for himself, then pulled out a small bowl and filled it for Repeat, leaving it on the counter.

"Come on, girl. Have some yum-yum," he coaxed to the finicky cat who hopped up on the counter and circled the bowl several times before dipping her delicate tongue in.

"Travis, you know that your mother doesn't like that cat on the kitchen counter."

"I know, Aunt Emma, but we're not going to tell her are we?" He winked. "Besides, if I put the milk on the floor, old Pete here would finish it off in one gulp."

Emmaline handed him a plate with toast and preserves as he walked past her to the breakfast room table.

"I don't know about that, Travis. We girls are quite capable of holding our own in a pinch, aren't we, Repeat?"

Emmaline sauntered over to join her nephew at the table, picking up a couple of napkins on the way. "Here, son. I honestly don't know why you young folks have such a problem with manners these days. One should never sit down to eat without a napkin in one's lap."

"Yes ma'am," Travis said with a humble smile, thinking to himself that he was more than glad to humor this sweet little lady who had brought such joy to their home. He quickly picked up the new edition of *The Village Voice*, hoping to catch a few lines before his great aunt had time to express her well-known feelings about reading at the table.

"Well, well, would you look at this," he exclaimed. "Old Sam's got that dude's picture plastered on the front page; you know - the one we kind of identified the other day."

"Let me see that," Emmaline Harris responded with a look of concern on her face. Reaching for the paper, her heart slowly began to ache, as the surly face of her former student stared back at her. The headline stated, "Accused Murderer Seen Around the Area," and the article went on to claim that he was a suspect in area drug activity.

"Well, I don't believe a word of it," snapped Aunt Emma, "and Sam Penton ought to know better than to scare the good citizens of this town with such heresay. I'll just have to speak to him myself about his poor choice of headline articles. Now, I will just put this away. After all, you know that the table is no place for reading."

Emmaline Harris abruptly changed the subject then as she exclaimed, "Oh Travis, look outside - there by the planter of Impatiens. What a lovely ruby-throated hummingbird. Did you know that their little wings beat up to hundreds of times per second? And, they are the only birds that can hover in one place, fly backwards or forwards, and, amazingly, fly up and down too. I just love this time of year when they come through our area in such abundance, on their way to Mexico and Costa Rica.

"I read somewhere that it takes them up to twenty-four hours to cross the Gulf of Mexico, and they have to double their normal body weight of three grams in order to be able to make the trip. I guess that kind of explains their greedy little attitudes around the feeder. You just watch; in a minute another one will come flying in and attack the one already at the planter. They are so....oh, see.....here come two more." Her eyes danced with glee as she anticipated the show.

"Man! That little buggar's holding his own," Travis responded with almost as much enthusiasm as his aunt.

"You made me learn all about them when I was nine years old. Remember? It was the summer that you and Uncle Harry rented that cottage at Mexico Beach for the month of August, and me and Trish spent a week with you."

"Trish and I," Emmaline corrected.

"Oh boy," he thought. *"She's in one of her 'very proper' modes this morning. Man, it's amazing how selective her hearing still manages to be."*

Out loud he said, "Right. You know, Aunt Emma, I really think that was when Trish first developed her interest in Science. Me too, but not enough to major in the stuff.

"I remember you and Uncle Harry took us on those nature walks, and we got to use his prized binoculars to watch the birds and butterflies. Man, that was fascinating to a nine year old kid. You explained to us all about migration, and we saw the Great Blue Herons and Peregrine Falcons on their way to Central and South America. But the thing I remember that fascinated me most was the orange and brown Monarch butterfly that you said flies thousands of miles in the fall to reach a warmer climate. You told us that it wasn't important that his wings were smaller and weaker than those of the larger creatures. You said that he had an unwavering sense of direction and purpose, and God would supply the necessary strength and guidance. You know, Aunt Emma, that lesson has stuck with me since then, especially this last year in college since Dad's death."

Emmaline Harris had been listening carefully to make sure that she didn't misunderstand a single word. No, she was absolutely sure that her normally reserved, stoic young great-nephew had just truly opened up to her for the first time since she had moved in.

"Why, Travis Whitestone, that just goes to show that one never knows when others might be watching and learning from something that one has to say. Thank you for telling me this. I will add it to my treasure chest of special memories."

Somewhat embarrassed, Travis shrugged and wondered fleetingly if his loose tongue was a result of spending so much time with Rachel this summer.

The new phone on the kitchen counter rang with a louder than usual sound, sending a disturbed Repeat sprawling from her post with an indignant "meow."

"Remember Aunt Emma; don't answer it until you check the caller I.D. box. If you don't recognize the number, write it down and let the recorder answer," Travis reminded her. "It's probably Rachel, though. She was supposed to call me sometime after 8:00 this morning."

His aunt, not happy about changing her ways, frowned as she read the number on the box. "Travis, is Rachel's number 653-9100?"

"No ma'am, and I don't recognize that number, do you?"

"Oh, I don't know," she said in a frustrated voice. "I can't remember everybody's numbers. You know I don't call that many people. Why, it could be just about anyone's."

"My point exactly," Travis responded. "If you don't know for sure, it's better to be cautious. If it's a legitimate caller, they'll leave a message, and you can call them back... Listen, here's the beep now."

"Hello; this message is for Mrs. Harris. This is Velma down at the shop. I was wonderin' if you could come on in a little early this mornin'. Mrs. Morgan canceled her 9:30 appointment, and I thought you might want it. Just give me a call at 653-9100."

* * *

The bells jingled on the front door of the beauty parlor as Emmaline Harris slowly shuffled in, waving good-bye to her nephew who was holding the door.

"Thank you so much, dear. I"ll see you around 11:30."

"11:30 - sounds about right," Velma thought. Mrs Harris usually liked to stay around for a few hours to chat.

Velma hurried over to offer Mrs. Harris some help. Sometimes the little lady would graciously accept, while at other times, she would almost appear to be insulted.

"Mornin', Mrs. Harris. Good to see you. How about some coffee?"

"Why thank you, Velma. Half a cup would be lovely. I seem to remember that your coffee is usually quite strong, so I will have one sugar and two spoons of the cream substitute, please."

A smile appeared on Velma's face as she fixed Emmaline's coffee.

"It's amazing," she thought, *"how that little lady with her bent, arthritic body can manage to appear so regal, like the Queen Mother or something. But for all of her proper language and ways, she can sure down 'n dirty gossip with the rest of us."*

"Here you go, Mrs. Harris. Make yourself comfortable while I mix up your hair color."

"Now Velma, don't you get it too blue. Last time I left here looking like my whole head was bruised."

"Yes ma'am, I'll keep that in mind. I sure am glad that you could come on in early. That Mrs. Morgan called before 8:00 this morning all upset soundin' and said she just couldn't make it in. Didn't give a reason. Oh well, she's a strange one I say - always seems troubled."

"You've seen some trouble with a stranger, did you say?" Emmaline asked. "That's very interesting. There seems to be a lot of that going around. What kind of trouble, Velma?"

"No ma'am; I said - well, never mind. Let's get you on back to the hair washin' station."

"Just one minute, dear, while I take another sip of coffee which, by the way, is exceptionally good this morning. I also need to remove the bobby pins from my hair. I don't want to lose them, you know. I'll just put them in my purse.

"It seems like I have to buy new packs of bobby pins much too often these days," Emmaline continued. "Velma, have you ever wondered where all of the lost bobby pins and missing socks go in this world? They seem to vanish with regularity, never to be seen again. But we all know that they have to be somewhere, now, don't we?"

"Yes ma'am; I mean, well no ma'am, I never thought much about it, but I'm sure you've got a real good point, you being such a smart lady and all." Velma tested the water with her wrist and again urged Mrs. Harris to come on back for her shampoo. After all, Mrs. Harris might have plenty of time, but Velma didn't have all day. Now that the new girl had walked out on her, she was short-handed again. You just couldn't get good help these days - and this one had seemed so promising.

Come to think of it, Beverly had not really walked out on her. She just hadn't shown up all last week - sort of vanished like Mrs. Harris' bobby pins. Wouldn't even return her phone calls. 'Course that kid who had answered the phone several times might not have given her the message either. Oh well—

Finally Emmaline was settled in front of the mirror, and Velma started gently combing through the thin blue-gray wisps of hair.

"Is the color all right for you Mrs. Harris?"

"Oh yes, dear, it's much better."

"Good, I've been takin' some more classes in hair colorin' over at the technical college this summer. I've sure learned a lot."

"Yes, I can tell. Do your classes have something to do with those meetings that have kept you so busy lately?"

"Oh, no ma'am. Those are my revival meetings out at the campgrounds. They started at the first of the summer and were s'pose to last one week. But the people just kept comin' and wantin' more, and the preachers said they would keep on having them as long as the people came. I try to go at least once a week, sometimes more when Billy's on the road."

"Oh? I've been meaning to ask you what line of work Billy is in, Velma."

"He's an independent trucker - has his own 18 wheeler. He contracts out on individual jobs. Sometimes he's gone for weeks at a time which don't bother me much. I can always find plenty to do."

The bells on the door jingled again, announcing the arrival of Mildred Vickery for her 10:30 appointment.

"Morning Mildred," Velma called. "You're early, but come on in and visit with us. I'll be with you soon. Grab yourself a cup of coffee."

Mildred was never one to miss out on a little chit-chat, and if truth be told, she usually came early by design to feast on any interesting tidbits that might come her way.

"Well, I sure hope you're going to have time to wax these chin hairs for me," Mildred said with a huff. "You know, I still say that my body's got things backwards. The older I get, the less hair I have on my head, but I sure keep gettin' more on my chin! Explain that.

"By the way, where is everyone this morning?" she asked as she surveyed the room. "Has Claire Morgan already gone?"

"No" Velma answered. "She called in early this mornin' all upset about something - canceled her appointment just like that without a fine howdy-do or anything."

"Hmph! I'm not surprised," Mildred responded with an air of conspiracy. "You know, strictly off the record, of course, I heard that she and that smooth husband of hers don't get along so good. He never comes to church with her; just her and that pretty daughter come. And that Claire, well she always looks unhappy. Never says much. If you ask me, somethin' ain't right in Dixie."

"My feelings exactly," Velma agreed, getting caught up in the spirit of a promising gossip session.

"You girls speak up now," Emmaline said, sitting up as straight in the chair as her little body would allow, and straining her neck toward Mildred in order to hear better.

"Mrs. Harris, you need to turn your head toward the front for me now, so I won't give you a crooked cut. Don't you worry; I'll make sure that you don't miss anything," Velma offered.

"Y'all heard about the body they found washed up out near 98, didn't you?" Mildred continued, on a roll now. "Well, I've got it through the grapevine from a very reputable source, mind you, that they've made an identification. It's a man from Panama City who's been missin' for over a year. Used to run a bingo parlor over in St. Joe. It looks like he was shot. And guess who they've been questioning? Ol' Smitty himself."

Just as Mildred was about to expound further, the front door burst open, and Velma's husband, Billy, came storming across the room.

"Velma, I've told you not to mess with them flamingoes out front. I had then turned just like I wanted them."

"Oh yeah? And which way was that this time, Billy?" Velma countered, never taking her eyes off of her work. "Lord knows I can't keep it straight."

"It don't matter which way I put 'em, or when I do it. That's my business, and you leave them alone. Can't you get that past your ol' mop of died hair and through your thick skull?"

Turning around abruptly in her chair and almost causing Thelma to drop her scissors, Emmaline Harris spoke severely. "Young man, I heard that, and I'll have you know that my nephew turned that misplaced flamingo around this morning so that he would be facing the same way as all of the rest of them. Furthermore, he did so at my request. Now, I'll thank you not to intrude on my Saturday morning haircut again with such poor manners. Why, you should be ashamed of yourself talking to your wife in such a way. Especially in front of customers."

"Lady," Billy said with a cutting edge to his voice, "You mind your business, and I"ll mind mine." He stormed out, leaving three startled women with their mouths hanging open.

Velma was disgusted, Emmaline was indignant at being talked to in such a way, and Mildred had completely lost her train of thought.

Chapter 19

Children are our most valuable resources.
Herbert Hoover

Travis, true to his word, picked Emmaline up at precisely 11:30. As they walked out to the car, he noticed that the lead flamingo was, once again, turned facing the opposite direction from the other three.

"Wouldya' look at that," he remarked. "I swear I turned that bird around straight this morning. You'd think the thing was alive or something."

"I've asked you not to swear, son. It's not biblical, you know," Aunt Emma scolded. "And, for heaven's sake, don't touch that thing again. Why Velma's husband, Billy, was absolutely furious this morning when he discovered that we had disturbed his little arrangement."

"No way! Man, that's weird, because those things are usually all facing the same way," Travis said, shrugging his shoulders. "Why should her old man care anyway? It's Velma's shop, isn't it?"

The two stopped by the pharmacy on the way home for Emmaline to get her blood pressure medicine refilled. She grumbled as usual about having to take any kind of medicine at all. She had told that doctor time and time again that she could surely find a herbal remedy for blood pressure problems, given enough time. He had assured her that time was not something she had the luxury of playing with in this case.

"Well, good morning to you, Mrs. Harris."

Brenda Coggins, the friendly clerk behind the counter always enjoyed Mrs. Harris' Saturday morning visits, as the little lady usually had a delightful story or juicy piece of gossip to share. "I see you've just come from the beauty parlor this morning. I must say that Velma did a beautiful job on your color today."

"Thank you so much, dear. I told her that I expected it to be much better this time. Why, she had so much blue on my hair last month, I looked like an Easter egg."

"Oh go on with you, Mrs. Harris. You never look bad. My daddy says that you're one of the loveliest ladies in this town."

"Well, Brenda, coming from the sheriff himself, I consider that to be quite a compliment. It's too bad that I am a good twenty years his senior, isn't it?" Emmaline answered with a twinkle in her eye.

* * *

"Mommy, why is that lady's hair green? See mama; look at that place on the back of her head. Do ya' see it?" The little boy walking up the aisle with his mother tugged at her pants and pointed.

"Hush your mouth, Jody," the petite blonde with the dimpled chin scolded. "It ain't nice to point, and it sure ain't nice to talk about your elders like that. Lord, I sure hope that lady didn't hear you."

"What's a elder, huh, mom?" Jody called out, even louder. "Is that old lady one?"

"Shh," his mother hissed, clamping her hand over his little mouth. "Boy, why've you been askin' so many questions lately? Is that something else Uncle Jay's been teaching you?"

Emmaline, amused at the conversation going on behind her, turned to face the little boy and said, "Yes, young man; I most certainly am an elder and, I might add, I am very proud to be one. I imagine that you will be one someday, too. You see, an elder is a person who has lived for quite a long time, sort of like Santa Claus." Turning to his mom, she continued, "We elders have usually lived long enough to acknowledge that there is still so much more to know, and we have discovered that one of the best ways to find out is by asking questions, right mom?" she winked at the red-faced mother who was slightly more than a child, herself.

Extending her hand to the little boy, she said, "Now, young man, my name is Mrs. Emmaline Harris, elder, and I don't believe that I have had the pleasure of meeting you, yet. What is your name?"

Emmaline thought that she heard a stifled gasp from the mother as the little boy hesitantly reached out to shake her hand, looking at his mom as if seeking permission.

"Yes'm, Miz Elder, my name is Jody, and I"m five years old," he said, holding up five chubby little fingers.

"Well, it is certainly nice to know you, Jody. You are a very smart young man to know your numbers and colors already. By the way, what color did you say my hair is?"

Jody's young mother, quite embarassed at this point, spoke up quickly.

"Oh, Mrs. Harris, ma'am; I'm so sorry about that. You know how children are sometimes."

"Nonsense, dear. I think the child's honesty is refreshing. Children are generally much more truthful than adults, you know."

"Well, my goodness, Mrs. Harris," Brenda interrupted from behind the counter. "The little boy's right; there is a spot in the back of your head that is as green as it can be. It almost looks like spray paint. Why don't you come over here closer and let me see if I can tell what it is."

Emmaline moved slowly behind the counter, mumbling something under her breath about "that Velma". Brenda turned her around to face the perfume display on the wall while she took a brush and worked on the designated area.

"I declare, Mrs. Harris, if I didn't know better, I'd think you were getting ready early for Halloween, or something," Brenda giggled. "I sure believe this clump of green hair has been sprayed with that temporary stuff that the kids buy to color their hair for trick-or-treating. I know some of the teenagers were using it last week for a costume party at school. Did Velma do this to you?"

"Well, I suppose she did, that scatter-brained girl. Honestly, I sometimes wonder where her brain is; apparently it's hiding up under all of that red hair of hers somewhere. Yes, I seem to remember that she absent-mindedly picked up what she thought was an old can of hair spray, squirted a few puffs, and threw it in the trash before using a new can to finish spraying my hair.

"However, I do know why she was so distracted this morning, and I can't say that I blame her too much. It was that unfriendly husband of hers. He came in the shop acting in a most belligerent way, right in front of her customers. I must say that we were all in a poor state of mind when that man left.

"Now, Brenda, will this stuff come out?" Emmaline asked with dismay.

"Oh yes, ma'am. Just wet it good - better yet, go on and wash it when you get home."

"Hmph!" Emmaline responded. "I certainly don't have time to do either. I'm supposed to help Libbie with her dessert for supper club at the Roper's this evening, and I need to be out of the kitchen early because Trish and her little friend are cooking supper for Travis and Wes tonight. Oh, what a mess."

Emmaline turned back toward the counter, running her hands through the back of her hair.

"Mister Jody, I want to thank you for a most astute observation. If you —"

Looking around for the little boy to whom she was addressing her thanks, she quickly realized that he and his mother were nowhere in the store.

Chapter 20

As long as one keeps searching, the answers come.
Joan Baez

Travis' attempt at conversation during the short ride home from the drug store was met with only a "hmph" or two from his stone-faced aunt. Only yesterday his mom and sister had expressed concern that Aunt Emma had not been her usual, bubbly self recently. Truthfully, she had been rather surly off and on. Libbie and Trish had decided to concentrate their efforts on trying to accommodate their lovely little aunt, hoping that the mood would pass quickly.

Travis was inclined to agree. *"Hey,"* he thought. *"I figure she deserves a little "hmph" or two on occasion, especially at her age.... Shoot, if I had a green patch in my hair, it would merit more than a good 'hmph.'"*

On Saturday afternoon, in the midst of hobbling around the kitchen grumbling about flamingos and Halloween paint, Emmaline Harris lost her balance and almost fell, dropping a carton of eggs on the floor.

"Well, beaver dam!" she exclaimed. Trish stifled a smile and rushed over to help her great aunt who gratefully accepted her arm. Once she was steady, Emmaline angled her left shoe up just enough to examine the sole; next she checked the right shoe.

"I can't believe this," she cried. "I thought that I cleaned all that nasty bubble gum off of these shoes before I came in the house. It appears that I missed a whole glob of the mess in the arch of my right shoe. I suppose that I could have cracked my head wide open, just like those eggs, if I had hit the floor.

"Libbie, dear, I'm so sorry about the mess. Would you mind, terribly, cleaning it up? I seem to feel a little light-headed."

"Of course not, Emmie. You just go sit in Rob's chair and prop your feet up on the ottoman - without the gummy shoes, please," Libbie teased as she tried to hide her concern. "You can take the recipe for the flan with you and read the instructions out to me. We can whip it up faster this way with both of us working on it."

Trish helped Aunt Emma to the lounge chair and said she would clean her shoes for her later, after she finished setting the table for the dinner that she and Rachel were preparing.

"That's very kind of you, dear. By the way, Trish, do you have any idea what becomes of chewing gum once it is deposited on streets, lawns. etc?" Em asked. "I mean, other than the obvious, like clinging to shoes and tires. People must throw out thousands of pieces of gum a day. Is it biodegradable? Would little microorganisms be interested in eating it and breaking it down? It seems logical, with all of that sugar and substance from trees, doesn't it?

"I wonder just how long it stays sticky," she continued. "You know, I have a theory about this. I feel relatively sure that somewhere in this universe there's a giant glob of gum floating around with millions of bobby pins, paper clips and safety pins stuck to it. Too bad my shoe happened to find a piece that was still earthbound."

Trish giggled and said, "Gee, I don't have any idea, Aunt Emma. I never really thought about it. I do know that it can cause numerous problems for innocent, unsuspecting birds and animals who either step in it or get it caught in their fur, feathers or bills. If I find out, do I get extra credit?" she teased, giving Emmaline an affectionate hug. Trish winked at her mother, and they shared a conspiratorial smile of relief that Aunt Emma's sense of humor seemed to be returning.

At 6:30 that evening, Libbie knocked on her aunt's bedroom door. "Emmie, are you ready? Matt will be here in a few minutes to get us."

Hearing no response, she cracked the door and peeked in, where she found Emmaline propped up in bed on the heating pad.

"Oh Lib, is it already that late? I'm afraid that I dozed off; I only meant to rest my back for a spell. I must have pulled it more than I realized when I slipped this afternoon. I believe that I will just stay right here in my room tonight. You two go on without me and have a good time. You don't think that the kids will mind that I'm here, do you?"

"Of course not, Emmie. You know how big this place is. They will be downstairs at the other end of the house. They won't even know that you're here, and I'm certain that they won't disturb you.

"I'll tell Trish to bring you some supper in a few minutes. Then, you should take some aspirin and go on to bed early tonight. And don't worry about your heating pad; I'll come in and turn it off when I get home."

Libbie kissed her aunt good night and left the door slightly ajar as she left.

"You two have fun now, and stay out as late as you want," Emmaline called out as Libbie started down the stairs. "And don't worry about the heating pad, dear; I'll be sure to turn it off."

"*Ah-hah,*" Libbie thought. "*I think I see what is going on now. I just bet that mischievous little lady planned this whole thing so that I would have to go out with Matt by myself tonight. At least, I hope that's all there is to it. She did seem rather puny most of the afternoon."* She dashed off a quick prayer for her aunt's well-being, as she grabbed her purse and answered the door.

"Hi, Matt, come on in. I'll be ready in just a minute," she called over her shoulder as she went to find Trish. Matt followed her out to the deck, where Trish and Rachel were rather frantically trying to start a fire in the grill.

"Do you girls need some help?" he asked.

"Oh yes," they exclaimed in unison.

"Quick, Matt, before the boys get back. We don't want to hear their snide comments about the fairer species and all that," Trish said.

Libbie related Emmaline's situation to Trish, while Matt worked on the fire for the girls. All the while, she was thinking how nice it was that Matt seemed to fit in so easily, never pushy or overbearing, but at the same time, always willing to accommodate.

Travis and Wes returned from the store shortly after Libbie and Matt pulled out of the driveway. They put the drinks and steak sauce on the counter in the kitchen next to a large bowl of salad, colorful with a variety of fresh greens and ripe red tomatoes from the farmer's market. The kitchen smelled deliciously of homemade bread and baking potatoes, and the additional smell of steaks on the grill enticed Travis out to the deck where Trish and Rachel were swinging on the wooden swing as if they had been in control for hours. Wes, however, couldn't get past the salad, where he stopped long enough to stab a piece of tomato with a fork laying on the counter. As he started out the french door, the phone rang, and he stopped to get it.

"May I please speak to Miz Harris?" a child's voice asked, rather shyly.

"Well, I'm not sure where she is. I could go check, if you'll hold on." Wes, who was intrigued with the small voice, went on to ask, "Who should I tell her is calling?"

"This is Jody, sir. I'm five years old."

"You are, huh? How about that! I was five years old myself, one time," Wes chuckled. "Hold on, Jody, while I go..."

"Hello...hello?" Emmaline called into the upstairs receiver.

"Mrs. Harris? Is that you? This is Jody. Remember me? Mama said that I could call you."

"Jody, did you say? You'll have to speak up, son, because sometimes we elders have a hard time hearing on the phone."

Wes smiled, hung up the phone, and joined the others out on the deck.

"Ummm; those steaks smell great."

Trish came over and linked her arm through his. "Hope you enjoy them, big guy. Eat all you want tonight, because you'll be working it off for sure next week. Oh, who was on the phone?"

"It was some kid calling for your Aunt Emma... nice little guy; said he was five years old."

"What?" Trish said with a note of concern. "I don't know any children around here who would be calling her, do you, Travis?"

Travis admitted that he couldn't imagine who the caller would be. "Just one more weird thing around here as far as I'm concerned," he said.

"Yeah, well she must know him and his family too, because he told her that his mom said he could call her," Wes replied.

"What's wrong with you two, anyway?" he continued. "We're talking about a little fellow here, not some drug gang member. Hellooo; reality check. I think you're both over-reacting this time," Wes said, shrugging his shoulders and grabbing a hand full of potato chips.

"You're probably right, Wes," Trish said. "I need to take her supper up to her anyway, so I will just ask her who the kid was. You know how I am. There's no need to have it bugging me all night."

"Yeah, I know Sassy. If you didn't have something to worry about, you'd worry because you didn't have something to worry about," He teased, side-stepping the pinch aimed at his midriff.

Trish knocked softly before pushing Emmaline's door open. She was surprised to see her aunt sitting in front of her dresser mirror brushing her hair. "Aunt Emma, your hair already looks great. Why are you brushing it? Mom got all of the green out of it for you this afternoon. Besides, you ought to be relaxing in bed if your back is bothering you," she softly scolded. "Here, I've brought your supper."

Emmaline was most agreeable, climbing into her four poster bed and thanking Trish profusely, with more enthusiasm than Trish had seen in days. Although the change was a welcome one, Trish was more than a little curious about the reasons behind it. Could it have something to do with the little boy on the phone?

"There you go, Aunt Emma," she said, spreading the folding tray out over Emmaline's lap. "I hope this is what you wanted. Mom just said soup of some kind, and I added some of the salad that Rachel made for our supper. I'll bring you some coffee later if you want."

"Oh no, dear! I'm sure that I will be asleep in no time, and there's no need for you to come up again. I'll put the tray outside of my door in the hall, and your mother can get it when she comes home. You run along now and enjoy your friends."

"Are you sure that you don't want me to check on you later? I'll be glad to."

"Absolutely not. I don't want to be a bother to anyone. Just pretend that I'm not even here."

"Yes ma'am. Oh, by the way, Wes said that the phone was for you earlier - some little boy. I didn't know that you knew any children around here."

"Why dear, you know an old school teacher like me is bound to make some youthful friends from time to time. This is a precious little boy who I met in the drug store today. He was the little fellow who told me about the green patch in my hair. It appears that I made more of an impression on him than I realized." Emmaline chuckled. "Good night, dear," she went on to say, with a note of finality.

Chapter 21

One must never be in a hurry to end a day; there are too few of them in a lifetime.
Dale Rex Coman

Around 11:15 Saturday night, Matt walked Libbie up to the front door of her house. The lights were on throughout the downstairs, and Wes' truck was still in the driveway.

Libbie was uncomfortably aware that no male had walked her up to this front door since she and Rob had dated. Back then, one or both of her parents had almost always been awake downstairs, usually in the kitchen making pretenses of having a late night snack before going to bed. They had not fooled her for a minute.

She remembered fondly those night visits with her mom. Her dad would usually retire, once she was home, but she and her mom would often stay up for another fifteen to twenty minutes, during which time Libbie would tell her mom the highlights of the evening - the kinds of things that her mom would want to hear. Mary Virginia Borden had always delighted in anything that made her only child happy, and she had always looked forward to their little chats. Now, strangely, Libbie's almost grown children were the ones that were awake downstairs, though they certainly weren't sitting up waiting for their mother.

Fighting the sweet pain of nostalgia, and remembering also the kind gentleman at her side, Libbie turned and said, "I imagine the kids are watching a video by now. Would you like to come in for some coffee, Matt?"

"Truthfully? Libbie, I'm so full from supper, that I don't think it would be wise. Thanks anyway."

Matt put his hands in his pocket and looked down at his feet as he shuffled back and forth. Both were aware of the awkwardness of the moment.

"But," he ventured, "I really would like to sit in one of these rockers and enjoy this nice breeze for a few minutes." Sensing some hesitation on Libbie's part, he quickly added, "That is, of course, unless you're tired, and I would certainly understand. I probably ought to be getting on home anyway. You know, we preachers don't usually keep late hours on Saturday nights."

"Oh no, Matt – I could sit out here all night. In fact, I often come out after supper. But I was just thinking that I need to run in and get my insect repellent. This time of year, the mosquitoes love me."

Matt relaxed and smiled. "I just bet they do. Would you bring some out for me, too? I'm sure that I'm not as desirable as you," he said with a grin, "but when they find that you're unappetizing, they'll probably come after me next. I'll save you a place."

Libbie's feet felt lighter than usual as she hurried in to get the spray, and she murmured a quick prayer of thanks before calling out to the kids that she was home, sitting out on the porch.

"Okay Mom," Trish called back. "Wes and I are watching a movie. Travis and Rachel left about an hour ago, and Aunt Emma has been quiet as a mouse all evening."

Out on the porch, Matt was fighting a mixture of emotions. His divorce had been finalized almost three years ago, against his wishes from the beginning. He had tried in every way humanly possible to make things work out. He had been as supportive and loving as she had allowed him to be. However, in the end, she had left anyway.

Many of his parishioners had been quick to share with him their interpretation of scripture concerning divorce. Some had referred to Matthew 5:32, saying that every one who divorces his wife, except for the cause of unchastity, makes her commit adultery. Well, first of all, he did not divorce Barbara. She, with the help of some very slick lawyers, divorced him. Secondly, without a doubt, he knew in his heart that she had not been unchaste; she had just been consumed by the evils of a devastating drug dependency. In fact, he had often wondered if the divorce had not been her way of trying to spare him, actually distance him from the physical and emotional grief that she experienced daily in her struggle leading to her death.

He had alternately given his problems to God, then taken them back so many times, riding up and down on a roller coaster of doubts, fears, and the human desire to take control. The shaky ride ultimately had come to rest at the very feet of a loving, heavenly Father, who, he knew, had been at the controls all of the time. He had once again turned back to one of his parent's favorite assurances from the Bible, Philippians 4: 6 and 7, which would prove to remain a constant reminder in his life of God's perfect peace which surpasses all understanding.

And, yes, he had found a very special peace in this lovely little town, the kind of healing peace that could only come from God. Was he now playing with fire to consider allowing anyone but God back into his life? Was there even room? Or, was he using his relationship with

God as a defense, an excuse to protect his vulnerability, to ward off any more unnecessary heartbreak? There it was - that "human" thing again.

The strong smell of citronella announced Libbie's arrival. She was followed by a sleepy Repeat who was, obviously, quite perturbed at having been so rudely awakened. The cat rubbed against Matt's leg several times, yawned, and then hopped up into his lap where she stretched and licked her paws a few times before curling up into a furry ball.

"Well, what do you know? I've never been overly fond of cats, but this little lady's rather sweet, isn't she?" he said with a sheepish look.

"Yes, she is," Libbie acknowledged. "I hope you don't mind. She's been known to tame the fiercest cat doubters, including Wes and Pete. I'm afraid that you're in for it, Matt. If you've had any concerns about a female winning your heart, I better warn you that you might be in trouble." *Had she been able to sense what he had been thinking? No way! Divine intervention—?*

"In fact," she continued, teasingly, "You might as well relax and try to enjoy her brazen advances, because she has a real determined look about her tonight. I'm really surprised that she's not curled up at the bottom of Emmie's bed. That's where she usually is by now."

"Speaking of your aunt," Matt said, "I hope that you'll tell her how much I missed her company tonight."

"I'll be sure to tell her, Matt, and she'll be thrilled. She thinks that you're really special. I couldn't believe that she - a staunch, lifelong Methodist, visited Riverside Community Church last Sunday, all because of you. Not that it's a bad reason, of course. By the way, she said that Bob and Vicki were there. What a feather in your cap.

"She also said that your sermon was lovely, and she has insisted that I visit your church with her soon. Actually, I've been planning to, but as you know, Reverend Anderson has been a friend of my family's, going back to my grandfather's day, and we've been members at the Methodist Church forever. You know how these small town allegiances are...."

"Libbie, one of my strong beliefs as a minister has always been that I am in the business of bringing souls to God, not recruiting bodies to sit in my congregation." Matt turned his chair to face Libbie and held out his arms to be sprayed with the repellent.

"Now, back to your aunt, do you think that she would be interested in being a candidate for the "Biggest Mouth in Town" contest? Sam told me tonight that she has some great stories from her past that ought to be shared with the community. I would hope that she might consider it an honor to be asked."

"Oh Matt, I think that's a wonderful idea. She needs something to perk her up. This might be just the thing. She loves a good project, and she's almost through putting up the jars of tea that she promised you, so this would give her something else to do.

"That reminds me, anytime you're ready for the painting, let me know. And several of the other artists down at the studio have started the plywood fish faces to be put around town. They should be ready next week. This is such a cute idea."

"Well, I don't know about cute, but I do know that the enthusiasm so far has been great. Sam should have the ballots ready for the stores by next week, and he's going to do a big front page promotion in the newspaper. So far, Sam, Jimbo, and Big Soloman have agreed to run. Sam and Jimbo won't even give me a hint about their stories, although they have promised me that they will be family friendly. Big Soloman is planning to tell his favorite ghost story about the moss lady, and I hear that it's a thriller - especially when he tells it. Now, if your Aunt Emma joined them, we would have ourselves quite a group."

Conversation was easy as they reviewed other topics of interest from supper club: the delicious Mexican theme meal, the interest in Matt's new, soon-to-be-completed home, the excitement over a mysterious celebrity rumored to be coming for the Seafood Festival and staying at the Hopkin's Inn (everyone was trying to guess who it was, but Jimbo and Shelley were remaining very secretive), and the recent mystery surrounding the Morgans.

Everyone had been sorry to learn that the body that had washed up in the tornado had been identified as Vince Morgan's half brother, Edward Parker. It now appeared that Vince had moved his family to the area for the sole purpose of trying to find his brother who had been missing for over a year. However, once the identification had been made, he had managed to keep the news from his wife and daughter, as well as others in the area, until recently. His reasons remained to be explained. Since the two men did not share the same last name, very few people had any reason to make the connection.

According to George and Fran, the authorities suspected a connection between the murder and the drug operation that was currently under investigation in the area. Libbie, amazingly, was able to put aside her grief and join in the group's expressions of outrage. They all agreed that it was time for their community to rid itself of these unwelcome criminals, and they spent considerable time discussing ways that they might help. A suggestion that had met with some approval concerned the formation of neighborhood watch groups which, throughout the country, had proven successful in deterring robberies and break-ins. However, someone mentioned that the more serious crimes seemed to have tapered off, if not actually stopped during the last couple of months, and they resented having to consider such a plan. Why, until recently, no one in Apalachicola even locked their doors during the day.

"Y'all should have heard the whittlers discussing this very thing yesterday morning at the Hardware store," Jimbo had recalled with a chuckle. "Old Mr. Hankins pretty much summed it up when he said, 'Looks like we've dodged a bullet around here and remained within spittin' distance of sanity.'" Everyone had laughingly agreed with Mr. Hankins' conclusion, and the conversation had switched to a lighter, more enjoyable and productive topic - the Seafood Festival.

Matt gave up his attempt to rock in the old wooden chair, his long legs proving to be a hindrance. Instead, he crossed one leg over the knee of the other, careful not to disturb the sleeping Repeat, and reclined slightly, taking advantage of a temporary lull in the conversation to relax and enjoy the sounds of the evening. Next to him, a relaxed Libby rocked gracefully, her legs also crossed and the toe of her left foot barely reaching the floor as it lightly pushed the rocker back and forth. She leaned her head against the back of the chair, closed her eyes and hummed softly. Matt found himself staring - intrigued with the slow, hypnotic rhythm as well as the lovely, peaceful vision she presented. Becoming uncomfortable with his thoughts, he quickly initiated more conversation.

"Did I tell you about the young man who came in the church last week looking for a job?" Matt said. "His name's Rex, and he's fairly new to the area - a drifter it appears, but he seems to be a quiet, hard worker. We just happened to need someone on the kitchen staff, and he didn't mind pitching in. Said he did quite a bit of K.P. in the navy before getting an honorable discharge. He didn't tell me much more about his past. He's pretty close-mouthed, almost seems sad a good bit of the time.

"Anyway, he's going to help me put out the signs and ballots for the festival. The really interesting thing is his transportation. He rides around on Jimmy John's old bike. And I tell you, that thing looks almost as good as new since those two worked on it. He says Jimmy's the one who told him to come talk to me."

Libbie smiled and was about to comment when she heard what sounded like footsteps in the side yard. They were slow and deliberate, and one look at Matt revealed the mutual concern on his face. His mouth formed a silent "shh," and he put up his hand, indicating to Libbie to stay where she was. He carefully removed Repeat from his lap and set her on the floor, before he stood and cautiously made his way to the end of the porch to investigate.

"Why Ms. Harris, what are you doing out here in the bushes this time of night? You aren't out here spying on Libbie and me, are you?" Matt teased, his relief obvious. "You'll make me feel like a teenager again."

Libbie, absolutely horrified, immediately rushed down the front porch steps.

Emmaline, with a determined look on her face, came slowly from behind the hydrangea bushes and headed toward the front yard, straightening her sweater and brushing the leaves off of her sleeves.

"Now, Libbie," she cautioned, holding up her hand. "I don't want to hear any fussing, dear. I know that I should be upstairs in bed, and I have a very good explanation. I just needed to take a little walk to ease my stiff back, and I didn't want to disturb the kids, so I let myself out the front door earlier when they were on the deck. I've had a perfectly delightful evening, and I feel much better. Now, I believe that I will take Repeat and head up to bed."

"But Aunt Emma, do you know how dangerous —"

"Yes, dear, and I love you soooo good for caring," She winked and patted Libbie on the arm before making her way up the steps with surprising agility. Matt met her by the front door with Repeat in his arms.

"Thank you, kind sir," she said with a theatrical nod of her head and a beguiling smile. "And good night to you both. Mind you, don't stay out in this night air too long," she admonished.

Libbie, clearly unhappy with such a brief explanation and abrupt dismissal, started to follow, but Matt reached out for her arm and pulled her back.

"Let her go, Libbie. She may not have given us the full story, but at least she's safe and at home, and I must say that I don't know when I've seen her looking so pleased with herself."

Turning Libbie around to face him, Matt continued, "You said that all of you have been worried about her. Well, it looks like to me that she may be getting back to normal...I guess; actually, what is normal for Ms. Emmaline?"

Libbie resisted a compelling urge to lean into the comforting arms whose hands still gently held her shoulders. Instead, she looked up into Matt's face and giggled. "Normal? Emmie? Matt, the two words hardly go together! When God created her, I'm sure He decided that she was so wonderfully unique, that He threw away the mold."

Matt smiled and simply stared at Libbie for several seconds before responding. "Lovely lady, I think I had better leave now. I have a sermon to preach at 8:30 in the morning."

With that, he let go of her arms, opened the door for her and thanked her for a very nice evening.

Chapter 22

No thank you, I'll walk; I'm much too old to ride!
Kathryn Hepburn

Monday morning came quickly, much to Trish's dismay. She had arranged to take the day off from work to spend the morning with Wes before he left, and she was up before 6:30, boiling eggs and cutting up fruit for a picnic brunch. The night before, she had made his favorite sweet tea with mint from Aunt Emma's rapidly healing garden.

Emmaline, like her garden, also seemed to be improving, almost mysteriously so. She had spent all afternoon Sunday bustling around the kitchen like a mother hen, with the energy of someone half her age, making a pound cake plus four dozen oatmeal cookies for Wes to take back to school. This was quite an improvement over the dozen chocolate chip cookies that she had sent with him the previous year. She had quickly explained that he was to share them with Soloman and Ella's nephew, George, who would be a freshman in the football dorm.

When Wes arrived to pick up Trish, Pete and Emmaline met him at the front door, Pete wagging his tail, and Emmaline carrying her purse.

"Good morning, Wes. I was just leaving. I'm so glad that I didn't miss you. I have left your cake and cookies on the kitchen counter."

"Thanks, Aunt Emma - and I promise I'll share some of them," he said with a wink and a quick hug. "You're coming over for one of my games this year, I hope."

"Of course, Wes. I wouldn't miss it. Be sure to send us some tickets as soon as you get them. You know that I prefer one of the earlier games before the weather gets too cool."

As she adjusted her hat and started out the door, she called back over her shoulder. "And don't forget that the Seafood Festival is planned for the first week in November. I hope that you are going to be able to come, dear."

He smiled at the sight of the little lady hobbling down the sidewalk, determination in every careful step.

Wes and Pete found Trish in the kitchen closing the picnic basket. She swatted Wes' hand away from the container of cookies on the counter. "Hold off, Wes. Those are for you to take later. Don't worry; I have some packed for you in the basket."

"But Sassy, I'm starving. I don't know about this brunch thing. I mean it's a nice idea, and all, but I'm not used to going this long without breakfast. I hope you've got a lot of food in that thing, if it's supposed to count for breakfast and lunch."

The day was beautiful, with a slight breeze coming in over the water and puffy cumulus clouds scurrying northward in an otherwise clear, blue sky. Wes and Trish strolled along hand in hand, lost in their conflicting thoughts - the pain of separation mixed with the excitement of finally reaching their senior year. They had not yet announced an official marriage commitment, but the fact seemed to be a foregone conclusion, something that they enjoyed playfully discussing.

"Wes, is that Repeat following us? Look, over in the monkey grass by the sidewalk."

Wes stopped and turned to his left, just as Repeat sprang out of the shrubbery and playfully latched on to his leg. This was one of her favorite games, and Wes had only recently come to accept that it was a harmless gesture on her part, especially since her front paws had been declawed. However, she remained quite sneaky, with hunter instincts prevailing, and one never knew when or where she might be lurking.

"Repeat!" Wes yelled as he shook the pleased cat off of his leg. "Dadgum cat. You're gonna grab hold of the wrong leg one day, and somebody's gonna kick you to China and back."

Trying to hide her amusement, Trish knelt down and scratched the unrepentant cat under her chin. "Repeat, what are you doing three blocks from home? I had no idea that you were following us all this way. Bad kitty! Now, what are we going to do with you?"

"Hey Trish," Wes fumed. "I hope you're not planning to bring that stupid cat with you when we get married. I mean, she's okay from a distance. But this pouncing on people's legs - man, that drives me crazy."

"Oh, poor baby, did she scare you?" Trish consoled teasingly, as she stood up and rubbed her hands across the stiff sprigs of his new flat top which had been recently cut for football practice. "What if she insists on coming with me, like today? Does that mean that you'll leave me standing at the altar?"

"Hmm, probably so, Sassy; I'm not looking for a package deal, you know." Wes answered with a twinkle in his eye. "Hey, I think you've over-rated yourself in Repeat's eyes anyway; see - over there by the boats. Looks to me like she may have been following someone besides you this time."

Trish followed his stare, and her eyes came to rest on a small, stooped figure, with a dark pillbox hat balanced on her blue-gray hair, a light shawl gathered around her shoulders, and her little feet sporting black, lace-up shoes with chunky square heels. Her purse was in one hand, while her other hand used her umbrella like a walking cane, bearing a striking resemblance to an elderly Mary Poppins.

The little lady carefully made her way across the uneven boards of the charter boats dock before stopping at an unmarked door to a small, shabby wooden building. She glanced hesistantly over each shoulder before knocking, and scurried in quickly when the door was cracked open.

"Wes...that was Aunt Emma. She told me that she was going to visit Sam Penton this morning. I can't believe that she wouldn't tell me the truth. She's always been such a stickler for honesty. What in the world do you think she's up to?"

"I don't know, Sassy, but you're probably getting all worked up about nothing again. I'm sure there's a good explanation. There usually is when Aunt Emma is involved. Let's just give her the benefit of the doubt. Why don't we go on across the street to the park and eat in a place where we can keep an eye on the building. It's pretty obvious that she doesn't want anyone to know what she's up to, so let's just lay low, and if she leaves soon, we'll go investigate."

Trish reluctantly agreed and picked up her cat. "OK, let's go to that table by the bushes where Repeat can play, and we can be partially hidden," she said.

Over an hour later, Emmaline Harris left the small brown building with a smile on her face and a spring in her short little steps. She never saw the young couple as they quickly packed up their gear and headed for the small shack. Repeat, who ran on ahead of them, was intrigued with the fishy smell of the area, but didn't stray too far because of the dock cats who hissed their warning claim to the territory.

Reaching the door, they knocked several times to no avail. Finally, Wes nudged the door open a few inches and called, "Hello?"

When there was no answer, they cautiously made their way into a dimly lit room, the only furnishings being a few rusty metal folding chairs and a wobbly wooden table. The back door was standing open, and no one was in sight.

They hurried back out into the sunlight, Trish relishing the fresh air and brightness after the musty odor of the little shack. She started to speak, but stopped abruptly and pulled Wes behind the little building. She pointed to the store front next to the end of the dock where they were standing. There stood Aunt Emma, chatting gaily with who else but Sam Penton. Repeat was nudging back and forth against her legs, and when Emmaline failed to properly respond, the indignant cat headed back toward Trish and Wes.

"Shoo, shoo, Repeat!" Trish whispered, waving her hand at the pesky cat. "Go back to Aunt Emma." However, at this point, Repeat was no longer paying attention to her owner; she had found the picnic basket which was much more interesting.

Wes pulled out of town at exactly four o'clock. He had spent a few hours with his parents before picking up his fifteen year old sister at school. This was Allison's first year at Apalachicola High, and anytime her legendary brother came around, she glowed with pride, not to mention the extra attention it brought her way.

After telling his family good-bye, he stopped back by Trish's. They sat in the truck and made plans to meet Sunday afternoon when she and Travis would be in Tallahassee taking Rachel to catch her flight to Miami. They also briefly discussed whether to confront Aunt Emma about the morning's escapade, and Wes said that he thought Trish should leave it alone.

"But Wes —"

"Shut up, Sassy," he said, with a familiar soft pinch to her nose. "You're gonna do whatever you want to anyway, so let's don't waste our time arguing about it."

Trish took his pudgy face in her hands and pulled it over to her. "Make me, Baby Face."

* * *

On Monday evening, Rex Parker rode his bike quietly through the back streets of town, avoiding neighborhoods and traffic as much as possible. Around 8:00, he pulled up behind Velma's shop and hid his bike in the bushes. After watching for a few minutes to make sure that no one was around, he worked his way over to the dumpster and turned on a small flashlight. He methodically began to pull out one box at a time and carefully check the contents, combing through the packaging noodles and paper before dumping the rubbish back in the dumpster and stacking the boxes next to it.

He was about halfway through when, suddenly, someone grabbed his right arm, pulling it behind his back. At the same time, the attacker wrapped his other arm around Rex's neck, squeezing so tightly that he thought his eyes would pop out

His left arm flailed helplessly in the air, as he tried to free himself. Hot air blew on his neck and a husky voice whispered in his ear. "OK, Bozo, you wanna tell me what you're doin' out here? Looks to me like you're up to no good."

The grip around his neck relaxed slightly, just enough for him to gasp a few short breaths before it tightened again. The voice continued... "Now, you wouldn't just happen to be one of Scotty's buddies, would you? Maybe looking for some more of that gutter stash that you guys so generously shared with me not long ago?"

The arm jerked his neck backward, and Rex felt his throat begin to close as beads of sweat covered his face.

"Aw, look at that," The deep voice growled in his ear. "The bozo has feelings. Whadya know?"

As Rex tried to figure out what to do next, he was turned around and slammed against the concrete wall of the shop, the stranger's arm mashed solidly against his adam's apple. A thin, scrappy but muscular young guy with short, blonde hair and wire rim glasses was inches from his face.

With his other arm, Jay, the attacker, fished a small flashlight from his pocket. He held it up under his chin and turned it on, revealing an ugly snarl.

"What's th' matter, wise guy; cat got your tongue? Don't you recognize your old friend? No, I guess you wouldn't. Yeah, I have a new look these days. Nice change, huh?

"Hey, you're not so sharp after all, are you?" Jay sneered. "Especially when your buddy ain't along holdin' your hand."

Rex pulled at the arm under his neck, attempting to catch his breath.

"Hold on, man!" - cough - "You've got the wrong person—"

"I don't think so, dude," Jay said. "Hey, let's see if we can't jog each other's memory a little bit here."

Jay shined the small beam of light on Rex's face, and in that instant he knew, without a doubt, that he was staring into the face of a perfect stranger.

Turning off the light, Jay took a deep breath and tried to mask his confusion as well as disappointment. In the same tough voice, he said, "All right, man, speak up. Come on; I ain't got all night. Who are you, anyway, and what were you doin' in Velma's dumpster? And this better be good...I hear it ain't your first visit."

Chapter 23

For straying dogs and Christians, there's no place like home.
                              Roberta Messner

Summer's end brought with it some delightful beginnings, one of the most exciting being the official start of the first "Biggest Mouth in Town" contest.

Matt, who had finally moved, but was far from being settled, was planning a kick-off party in his new home, and he had asked Libbie and Mildred Vickery to serve as co-hostesses, thereby avoiding any speculative comments from wagging tongues. He was actually very proud of himself. This allowed him to discreetly involve Libbie, while Mildred, the chief gossipmonger in town, would also be appeased with her inclusion. He had invited all of the festival committee board members, the events chairmen, the four "biggest mouth" contestants and their respective spouses.

Emmaline Harris had been thrilled when asked to be a participant, and she had unofficially started her campaign weeks before the kick-off party, as she had solicited the full support of the garden club, promising numerous herbal benefits to the members. In addition, she had become quite the gad-about in town, charming the old-timers as well as the younger citizens with her grandmotherly ways and chocolate chip cookies. No one would dare accuse the little lady of bribery, and, besides, no rules had yet been established governing the contest.

It was not unusual these days to see the green and white Village Public Regional Shuttle van pull up in front of the Whitestone house. Aunt Emma, who had throughout the summer enjoyed the chauffeur services of her niece and nephew, was thrilled with this wonderful new service which allowed her reasonable access to any part of town. In fact, she and Fred, the driver, had become good friends, and she had already ordered a can-collecting basket for his van.

"Now Fred," she had chided, "make sure that you remind all of your passengers to save their aluminum cans and put them in your basket. It's important to recycle, you know, and besides, you can redeem those cans for money. And Fred, you ought to use that money to buy voting slips for our contest...all for the good of the community, of course."

No one was surprised when a "campaign" poster of Emmaline Harris appeared on the wall of the small shuttle van. The picture featured the smiling, little lady, wearing a white, crisp eyelet-trimmed apron and bonnet. She was sitting in her famous rocker behind an old, foot-operated spinning wheel, winding threads from a hand-full of angora fluff. The caption under the picture read:

Ms. Emma certainly knows how to spin a yarn.
Vote for
EMMALINE HARRIS
BIGGEST MOUTH IN TOWN!

* * *

Friday morning, the day of Matt's party, was the promising start of a glorious, lazy indian-summer day, much welcomed by Trish. Travis had left the day before for Georgia Tech, and his departure had been anything but pleasant. He had lectured his three women about caution as if they were two year olds, instructing them to call Matt, Sam or even old Bernie if they noticed anything or anyone unusual around town, especially the dark-haired stranger that they had possibly recognized earlier in the pictures. Libbie had promised to keep in close contact with Matt; Aunt Emma had simply smiled and told Travis not to worry.

Two very long weeks loomed ahead of Trish, whose friends and brother were already back at school. She had completed her summer job the week before, and she decided to indulge herself on this lazy Friday morning by sleeping in late. Around 9:30, she stumbled into the kitchen. She poured a glass of orange juice and crawled into her dad's lounge chair in the breakfast room, enjoying the fresh air from the open windows while watching a mindless talk show about body tattoos.

"*Aah*," she thought. "*Life is sweet. Poor Travis is probably standing in some long registration line at school, with his mind back in Apalachicola, imagining all sorts of dangers lurking about out little village.*" In reality, the scariest things that Trish had seen lately were the weirdoes she was watching on television at the moment.

Her mom was painting over at the gallery this morning, and Aunt Emma was nowhere to be found, indicating that she was out somewhere hot on the campaign trail. The only other sign of life around the big house was Repeat, who came flying through her cat door from the deck and hopped up in Trish's lap just as a bearded, motorcycle gang member on TV was revealing a tattooed sunset spread across his rather large belly.

"Well hello, girl. Check out that sunset on the big guy's tummy - gross, huh? Hey, looks like we've got it all to ourselves this morning, doesn't it? Where's your pal, Pete?"

The cat was in no mood for petty conversation, as she attempted to sharpen her clawless front paws on Trish's terry cloth robe. She arched her back in a way that indicated she was thoroughly agitated. Then she quickly hopped down and flew over to the door, stopping and turning to look at Trish.

"Repeat, what is it, you spoiled cat? Can't you see I'm trying to relax? Go on out if you want to, but don't expect me to come play with you right now. Why do you think we put that cat door in for you?"

However, the insistent cat would not take no for an answer. She repeatedly alternated between Trish's leg and the door, until Trish finally got up and followed, wrapping the sash around her robe and grabbing her orange juice. No sooner had she opened the door than the skittish cat flew past her and down the steps of the deck, stopping at the bottom to look back and make sure that Trish was following.

"OK, girl, what's out there that's got you so worked up? A squirrel, maybe? Come on, let's go see."

At that moment, Trish heard another pitiful sound, the whimpering of a dog in pain. She rushed down the steps and followed Repeat to an azalea bush out in the yard, where she found Pete curled up in a bloody ball.

"Oh Pete, baby. What's happened to you?" she cried, as she knelt down to comfort and check the Cocker. His soulful, big brown eyes looked up at her, and he tried to wag his tail, but the obvious pain, which appeared to be coming from his right hip, turned the wag to a moan. The normally aloof Repeat gently nudged her head against the dog's side, as if trying to tell him to lay down.

Trish carefully probed the hip, feeling for fractures, and had no trouble finding a jagged break in the right femur. A nasty tear in the skin was bleeding profusely.

"It's all right, baby," she soothed, rubbing his forehead gently. "You stay here with Repeat, and I'll be right back." She took a second to also rub Repeat's soft, furry head and instructed the cat to stay with her friend.

For one paralyzing moment when she reached the kitchen, Trish was at a loss as to who she should call. She had become so dependent on Wes lately - especially after her father's death, and when Wes was unavailable, her brother had almost always been there when she needed him. She suddenly understood how alone her mother must feel at times, and her heart ached for her. At the same time, her heart was breaking for Pete, and she found herself dialing the number to Riverside Congregational Church as if it was a perfectly natural thing to do.

Doc Hastings himself was at the Whitestone's home in less than ten minutes after Matt called him. He gave the suffering Pete a shot to calm him down, and with Trish's help lifted him onto a stretcher.

"You're right, Trish. That's a nasty fracture, but it's not life-threatening. Truth is, I would have been more concerned about the loss of blood, but you did such a beautiful job of wrapping the area, that I think ol'Pete here is going to make it. Your dad would have been mighty proud, young lady."

Trish tried to stifle an unexpected sob in her throat, but not before an observant Matt noticed and put a consoling arm around her shoulder. "Let's don't call your mother yet," he said. "There's no need to worry her until after Doc patches things up. Why don't you ride with Pete and the Doc to the vet's office, and I'll follow. We can call Libbie when we have more to tell her."

"Thanks, Matt. I can't tell you how much I appreciate all of this. I hate to even ask another favor, but would you mind saying a little prayer for Pete on the way? I know he's just a dog and all, but I don't think we could handle losing him right now."

"Hey, little lady, praying's one of the things I do best, you know. And you know, God loves that dog just as much as you do. Now you go on with Doc, and consider it done."

Doc Hastings had concluded that the dog was probably hit earlier that morning by a fast-moving vehicle, and if Trish had not found him when she did, he more than likely would have died.

"Someone was definitely looking after the little fellow," he had told Trish and Matt. "Beats me how he even managed to get out of the street and up to that bush. You know, I just can't believe that someone would hit an animal like that and then leave. It makes me mad everytime I think about it. I've already called the Sheriff, because that could have been a child. Hit and run is the same in my book, whether it's an animal or a human. Good ol' Bernie has promised to keep an eye out for strange or careless driving vehicles in the area. In fact, Bernie said somebody reported a small, gray short-bed truck speeding through some of the neighborhoods this very morning.

Later that afternoon, a tranquilized Pete, sporting a complete hip to paw cast, lay contentedly in his new, flannel lined bed next to Repeat's area rug in the breakfast room. A vigilant Repeat guarded him carefully, allowing no one but Trish to come near him. She left her post occasionally to rub against Libbie and Aunt Emma's legs, as if to reassure them that she still loved them, but wanted them to take care of matters other than those involving Pete. Actually, Libbie and Emmaline did have another matter of concern that evening - the party at Matt's house.

The two ladies left around 5:00, as they had told Matt that they would come early to help with the food. They were worried about leaving Trish alone for the evening with all of them being out on the island, but Trish was insistent that she would be fine. Wes was supposed to call later, and besides, she assured them, she and Repeat had everything under control, promising that she would lock up tight when they left, and would call immediately if she needed anyone.

Chapter 24

*The world is so full of a number of things, I
think we should all be as happy as kings!*
                    Robert Louis Stevenson

As soon as Libbie's Honda turned the corner, Trish strolled out on the wide front porch and drank in the familiar sights and sounds of her cherished neighborhood, relishing the moment and trusting that its memory would sustain her through countless gloomy nights in her cramped, dingy apartment back at school.

Two houses down and across the street, several neighborhood boys were playing in a pile of sand by the side of the old, reportedly haunted Radcliffe house. An investor from Louisiana had recently purchased the decrepit mansion and was doing a first-class job of re-furbishing it to showcase splendor.

The house had been vacant since Trish was in Junior High School, and its rumored ghosts had been the thrill and fascination of many slumber parties and late night strolls. She vividly remembered the strange Radcliffe family, and she especially remembered the weekend when they had seemingly just disappeared.

Sally Radcliffe had been a shy youngster a year younger than Travis and Trish. The three had walked to and from school together for years, but Sally had never invited the twins in, and she would never leave her yard to come visit at their house. Some of the other neighborhood kids used to say that they heard weird moans and screams coming from the house at night, and it was rumored that Sally's father was beating Sally and her mother.

One weekend in early spring, it seemed that the family just vanished. Sally had not gone to school on Friday, and no one had seen any sign of activity over the weekend. But on Monday morning, the big house was completely vacant. The only evidence of the Radcliffes having ever lived there was a blurred message scribbled in crayon on a bathroom mirror upstairs. It had said,

"Please help me.."

A "For Sale" sign had gone up the next week, but the listing agent had only shown the house one time. According to her, it was on a Saturday evening, and a couple from out of town had been very eager to tour the large, stately home. The Realtor had carried them through the home, room by room, waiting uncomfortably as they had looked in every nook and cranny. They had finally ended up on the back verandah, where the view of the yard sloping gently down to the bay was fantastic, with palm trees swaying in the sunset and sailboats gliding sleepily by.

The couple had expressed quite an interest at this point, asking specific questions about price, appliances and warranties. The Realtor had been ready to pull out a contract when, all of a sudden, the back door had slammed, locking them out. The lights in the house had then proceeded to blink on and off, and a strange moan had been heard coming from upstairs. No Realtor or prospective customer had officially stepped foot in the place since then.

The bank had received regular monthly payments from an attorney's office in Seattle, Washington until the following December when the mortgage had been paid in full. Records showed that the deed had been transferred to the name of Sally Radcliffe, minor, Attorney Jonathan Sikes, legal guardian. The house had remained vacant for the next six years.

The neighbors were delighted with the recent purchase and on-going renovation, and Trish shared their sentiments. However, she would actually kind of miss the old relic. She looked forward to one day telling her children about the many ghost escapades that had been such an intriguing part of her wonder years......like the time that she and Travis had dared that mean old bully, Brad Hogg, to go in the garage behind the house. They had told him that they thought Sally's bicycle might still be there. After calling them "chicken twins," he had hesitantly ventured into the rotting, dilapidated old wooden structure through the creaky back door. Giggling, Travis and Trish had quickly closed the door behind him and secured the rusty hinge lock on the outside, after which they had pounded the tin roof with rocks and moaned "Help me."

They had then run across the street and hidden behind a car, watching until, to their delight, a screaming, pale Brad had crawled shakily out of the high window on the side of the building and run "bloody murder" down the street. He had never told anyone about the escapade because, first of all, the police strictly enforced the "No Trespassing" sign on the property, and secondly, he would never want to admit his cowardice.

Remembering the incident, Trish found herself giggling as much this evening as she had that day so long ago. What a shame that the little boys playing in the sand pile would never experience a good old Radcliffe haunting. Oh well; they would probably find ghosts of their own.

A movement across the street caught Trish's eye, and she waved at Grandpa Cleveland who was making his weekly preparations for his usual Saturday ritual. Years ago, after his back surgery, he had established a pattern of cutting his lawn in a methodical and precise way. Every Friday evening, tonight being no exception, he would fold out his lounge chair in the middle of the huge front yard. The next morning he would carry out a large thermos of lemonade and set it on the ground next to his chair. This always took place between 9:00 and 9:30 A.M. on Saturday. He would then go to the corner of the house and plug in his seemingly antique, although amazingly reliable, electric lawn mower. From the day that he had bought the unusual mower, Mrs. Cleveland had declared that he was bound to get electrocuted someday when he ran over the cord.

Next, Mr. Cleveland would mow around the outermost edge of the yard, unrolling the long series of extension cords as needed. After making two complete squares around the perimeter, he would shut off his mower, have a few sips of lemonade and promptly fall asleep in his lounge chair. The nap usually lasted for about thirty minutes, after which he would proceed to mow a few more square orbits before his next lemonade and nap break. He generally completed six to eight laps before going in for lunch and a ballgame on TV. Between 3:30 to 4:00, he would amble back outside, determined to finish the front yard before dusk - and, barring unforeseen circumstances, he usually did.

Mr. Cleveland waved back at Trish and called out, "Evenin' young lady. When are you going back to school?"

"I leave two weeks from Monday, Mr. Cleveland. Auburn is always the last school to start it seems," she answered. "Your yard sure is looking nice," she added.

"Thank you ma'am, but it'll look a heap better after I cut it tomorrow."

"Oh, yes sir. By the way, where is Bambi?" she asked, knowing perfectly well that Mr. Cleveland's thirty-nine year old daughter with Down's Syndrome would be inside watching Andy Griffith re-runs on TV - or possibly watching Wheel of Fortune at this time of evening.

Trish had always been Bambi's favorite baby-sitter - until recently when Mrs. Cleveland had died. Now Mr. Cleveland stayed home most evenings, and with Trish off at school, Libbie and Aunt Emma loved to have Bambi visit if Mr. Cleveland was in a pinch. This was seldom, however, as Bambi's two brothers and their families lived across the bridge and Bambi spent as much time in their homes as she did in her own. The Clevelands were a very close, loving family, and they were always quick to give Bambi the credit for teaching them about unconditional love.

Bambi was well-known around town and adored by everyone. Her full name was Barbara Marie Cleveland, but she had been called Bambi most of her life because of her captivating fawn-like features: silky auburn hair which was usually worn in a ponytail, large, almond-shaped, widely-spaced doe brown eyes that reflected innocence and pure love, a pert, little, flat pug nose, and a genuine trusting smile that melted even the hardest of hearts. Yet, this charming little imp was anything but reticent! She had a delightful and surprisingly quick sense of humor, a mischievous nature, and she was very much a take-charge person, inasmuch as she was able. On occasion this nature presented problems, as Bambi failed to recognize that she had any limitations.

Trish smiled as she rememebered the Saturday last summer when she had kept Bambi for the day while Mr. Cleveland went deep-sea fishing. The two of them had been making lunch, with Bambi setting the table while Trish pan-grilled the cheese sandwiches. The phone had rung, and by the time Trish had returned to the stove, the sandwiches were black and smoking. When the smoke alarm went off, Bambi had run from the room holding her ears. Trish hadn't thought too much about Bambi's quick exit (she had been more concerned with cutting off the alarm) until she heard the unmistakable whine of the fire truck sirens. Bambi, it turned out, had dialed 911. "I thought we were on fire!" she had explained, enjoying the excitement.

One of the young volunteer firemen - a teenage boy who was in training - had stared at Bambi with open curiosity. When the firemen had left, Bambi had run to the window, giggling. "Tish, Tish, did you see that boy? What's the matter with him - crazy or something? He was looking at me with a funny face....You know why? I think he likes me. Ooooh, Tish. He might want to marry me!" With that announcement, the precious little girl/lady had wrapped her short, double-jointed arms around her characteristic Down's plump torso and swayed back and forth singing, "Here comes the bride."

As he headed back toward the house, Mr. Cleveland called back to Trish, interrupting her thoughts.

"I imagine that Bambi's doing what she loves best, Trish - watching TV. I'd better go on in and check on her though. You have a good evening young lady."

The sky was beginning to darken, and the crickets and tree frogs were taking their cue as they began a tentative warm-up of their nightly serenades. The mosquitoes were also making their presence known, prompting Trish to turn toward the door as she slapped at one of the pesky creatures on her arm. The little boy on the sidewalk across the street must have thought that she was waving at him, and he eagerly waved back as he ran across to her yard. Trish saw his reflection in the glass panel windows which surrounded the front door, and she turned back at the sound of the child's voice.

"Hey ma'am; are you Ms. Harris' girl?"

"Well, in a way I am," Trish responded with a grin. "Actually, I'm her great- niece, Trish. And who are you?"

"I'm Jody Barineau, and I came to give Ms. Harris this here box. Is she home?"

The small boy was a picture- perfect Norman Rockwell replica, with shaggy reddish hair, green eyes, and freckles sprinkled liberally over his face. His wide smile was contagious, and he obviously had seldom met a stranger.

Trish walked over to the porch steps. "No, Jody," she said. "I'm afraid that Aunt Emma's not home. She's gone to a party this evening. But I'll be glad to give her the box for you. Would that be okay?"

Jody's grin faded slightly, and he glanced across the street at a man who was leaning against the telephone pole. He looked back at Trish and said, "Well, I don't know Miss Trish. Uncle Jay said I'm only s'pose to give it to Ms. Harris. Maybe I better ast him."

With that, he turned and ran, his sturdy little legs carrying him quickly across to the lanky, blonde-haired stranger slouched against the pole.

In a few minutes he was back without the box. "Uncle Jay said we would bring it back," he declared, and as children often do, changed the subject in the next breath. "Where's your doggie?"

"My doggie? Do you know Pete?" Trish asked.

"No ma'am, but I seen him in your yard before. Uncle Jay said to ast you if he was OK."

Glancing at the man with whom Jody had just consulted, Trish asked, "Is that your uncle across the street, Jody?"

"Yes'um, that's Jay, but he ain't really my uncle. I just call him that. He's my mom's frien' and he's real nice. He said your doggie might of been hurt, and he cares about doggies and kitties and things like that. He even picked a tic off my cat last week. Showed me how to do it too, 'cause my mom, she won't touch them things, you know."

Once again Trish looked uneasily across the street, noticing that the stranger's back was now turned. Something about his posture, or lack of it, made her uncomfortable. He was slowly pulling a little red wagon back and forth, and the mysterious box was sitting right in the middle of it.

She turned back to Jody, choosing her words carefully as she explained, "Jody, you're right; my doggie has been hurt. We think he was hit by a truck this morning. But the doggie doctor has fixed him up, and he's going to be fine. Now, can you tell me how your Uncle Jay knew about it?"

"No'm; he ain't told me. You want me to go ast him?"

Trish was hesitant to encourage further communication of any kind with the stranger. Travis' warnings rang in her ears, and she knew that the sensible thing would be to go in the house and lock the doors. Yet, she was intrigued with the little boy, who obviously had won Aunt Emma's approval. Besides, she really needed to find out what "Uncle Jay" knew about Pete's accident. What if he, in fact, had been driving the truck? Of course he would never admit to that, but it would be interesting to hear what he did have to say.

"Yes, Jody, if you don't mind; please do go ask him for me."

She winked at the precious child and offered a quick prayer for his well-being....as well as for hers. Surely the man, Jay, was a kind enough person if little Jody thought so much of him. Nevertheless, she edged closer to the front door, ready to scurry in if the lanky stranger decided to accompany Jody back across the street, making her more uncomfortable in any way.

Jody was back in a flash without Jay, who, Trish noticed, had already started pulling the wagon down the sidewalk toward the corner.

"Miss Trish," the little boy panted, winded from the many trips back and forth. "Uncle Jay says he come up on your little doggie in the street this mornin'. He ain't seen who hit it, but my mom was drivin' him to work, and he made her stop so he could check on the little feller.

"Says he picked your little doggie up and carried him out of the street so he wouldn't get hit no more. He put him in the shade by a bush in your yard. Well, that's all; I gotta go now. See ya' Miss Trish."

Trish called a sincere "thanks" to the small, retreating figure; she noticed that Uncle Jay was already down at the end of the street.

Chapter 25

*God is patient with the process. Think of the
enormous leisure of God; He is never in a hurry.*
O. Chambers

Bubbles was washing dishes when she heard the wagon wheels crunching on her gravel driveway. She looked out of the kitchen window, relieved to see that Jay, true to his word, had indeed brought Jody home before dark, although just barely. She smiled at the sight of Jay pulling the little red wagon while Jody rode piggy-back, yelling "yee-hi!" and swatting Jay playfully with his cowboy hat. In response, Jay broke into a gallop, almost slipping on the driveway rocks. The two of them laughed playfully as Jay stopped and knelt down on the grass, gently rolling Jody off of his back.

Bubbles glowed with the joy of the moment. *"It's almost like we're a real family,"* she thought briefly before disciplining her thoughts back to reality.

Back during the summer, she had allowed Jay to move into their spare room behind the garage. The arrangement had been acknowledged as temporary, but it now appeared to be settling into a comfortable, stable situation.

The room was actually an extra large storage/laundry room that had been added on by the previous owners. The front door of the room opened directly into the carport, which one must go through in order to enter the kitchen door on the side of the house. The other door opened to the back yard, and outside, to the right of this door, was a small, crude outdoor shower with a floor of widely-spaced slat boarding, enclosed on three sides with walls of white Formica panels nailed to a frame of two-by-fours.

The old gentleman who had lived in the house before had been an avid hunter and fisherman. His wife had adamantly refused to let him clean his fish and game in her neat, clean little house. Besides the mess, she complained, was the horrible smell. The fact that the old man often smelled as bad or worse than his catch of the day facilitated the need for the outside shower, along with the sink inside for cleaning his fish and birds. When he was fortunate enough to kill a deer, he let the boys at the camp take care of things.

The toilet inside next to the sink had been an afterthought, the decision made after the Mrs. had suffered a severe attack of asthma one weekend causing him to forfeit his Sunday morning cigar.

"A man's throne is his castle, don't you know?" he explained to the middle-aged, male Realtor who was showing Bubbles the house. "Now Mama, she had lots of trouble breathing and stuff, and so I just put me my own little throne right out here away from the house. That way I could enjoy my Sunday newspaper with a good old cup of coffee and a cigar, the way a man ought to. That little lady didn't complain too much, except on Monday mornings when she said she couldn't hardly stand to wash clothes 'cause they would smell like smoke. I tell you, she had a nose like a hunting dog. God love her; I sure do miss her. I don't reckon I'm gonna have much of a throne in the nursing home."

The day that Jay had moved in, Bubbles established some specific ground rules. "I don't allow no alcohol, tobacco, or drugs on my property. I see enough of that mess where I work, and I don't want to come home to it. Fact is, I'm gettin' myself out of that den of sin just as soon as the new restaurant opens in that resort on the island. I've been offered the head hostess position, in charge of the dining room. You see, I figure that it's real important where I work from now on, 'cause I've got a son to raise, and he'll be exposed to that stuff soon enough without his ma working around it.

"Another thing, if you're planning on staying out and keeping late hours, you best not come in here waking anybody up. We got us a quiet little home here, and I aim to keep it that way - and don't go askin' to borrow my car. I don't know how you get around, but it won't be in my car unless I happen to be going in the same direction.

"Now, you're welcome to take meals with us, but I'll expect you to buy some of the food from time to time. Just buy the stuff you like, and put it in the refrigerator or cabinet. Beverly, she does most of the cooking, and she can take about anything she finds and whip up something pretty good.

"I tell you, I don't know much about charging rent either. Bev just works hers out by cooking and cleaning and keeping Jody for me. I'd feel kind of bad charging anybody rent for that little back room you're in out there. Hey, how about you just keeping the grass mowed for me and we'll call it an even swap?"

Jay had quickly agreed and was thrilled with the living arrangements. *"Unusually so,"* thought Bubbles, making her wonder about a background that would make someone so grateful for an army cot to sleep on, orange crates for storage, and a clothesline rope strung from one corner of the room to the next for his few hanging clothes. This he shared with the rest of the household laundry. The remaining furnishings in the room included a washer and dryer, a broken cane rocker with the seat out, and an old dusty, mildewed steamer trunk that had belonged to Bubbles' grandfather.

Bubbles actually knew very little about Jay's background. She remembered that he had been cautiously close-mouthed their first night together, when they had sat on the blanket under the stars and listened to the revival music. Hoping to bring him out some, she had done most of the talking, sharing information and stories about her past, her family, and her current lifestyle. *"Why not?"* she had thought. After all, she had nothing to hide, did she? *"Did he?"* she had wondered.

Jay had listened with genuine interest, asking questions occasionally. Before the evening was over, he knew that she and her sister Beverly, had been born in Birmingham, Alabama, living there until their teenage years when their father, a railroad engineer, had failed to come home one week after a trip out west. The family had soon learned that he had been keeping a second wife in Oklahoma, neither wife knowing about the other until the Oklahoma spouse became suspicious and hired a private detective. Upon learning about his Alabama family, the second wife had issued an ultimatum, and Bubble's dad had chosen the younger and more attractive, not to mention, wealthier woman. As far as Bubbles, Beverly and their mom knew, he had never returned to Alabama.

Bubbles' already plump mother had suffered from severe depression, becoming so overweight that her health had been affected to the point that she lost her job. She and the girls had then moved down to Carrabelle, Florida across the bay from Apalachicola, to live with Uncle Charley, her mom's brother.

She fondly remembered Jay's comment that her parent's weaknesses must have made her determined to be their exact opposites. In fact, she was flattered when he told her, "Woman, I can already tell that you're real careful with your trustin'. You remind me of a feisty little old blonde poodle, real protective like and ready to bite the fire out of anybody that messes with you or your family. I don't reckon I've known many females like that."

It was true that she took pride in her trim, healthy body, unlike her mom. "As long as you have your health, you'll have the jump on a lot of other people," she always said. And there was no doubt that she was fiercely loyal and devoted to her family.

Bubbles made good money, especially off of tips at the Top Flight Lounge, and each month she gave some to her mother who still lived in Uncle Charley's trailer. On rare occasions, she received a pittance of child support from her ex-husband, when he was sober enough to hold down a job for any amount of time.

She allowed her sister to live with her, rent-free, in exchange for Beverly's baby-sitting Jody at night when Bubbles worked, and Beverly was eternally grateful for her sister's generosity. Beverly had suffered throughout most of her life with the crippling remains of childhood polio. She wore a leg brace on her right leg which helped her walk short distances. However, her job choices were limited, as sitting upright for any period of time was extremely uncomfortable with her brace on, and a job which required much walking was not even an option.

Beverly had recently completed Cosmetology School, hoping to be able to work part-time. Velma at the beauty parlor downtown had hired her immediately and had been very understanding when she needed to rest. Things had seemed to go well for a while. Beverly had even gone out several times with one of the customers - a traveling man who dropped in from time to time. Bubbles still wondered why their relationship had ended so abruptly.

"One day Beverly came home early," Bubbles told Jay, "crying and shaking so bad that I had to give her a tranquilizer and put her to bed. She wouldn't tell me what was wrong, but she ain't seen that man or gone back to work since then. That Velma lady called here looking for her a few times, but Beverly wouldn't talk to her or return her calls. Beats me as to what happened. I guess it's worked out all right though, 'cause she sets at home and works on her needlepoint that she sells at those Arts and Crafts Fairs. Some rich lady in town takes her stuff around to the shows for her, and whatever doesn't sell, that lady buys it herself. Gives Bev a little spending money, and it keeps her busy."

During the conversation that first night under the stars, Jay had asked her about her real name.

"What makes you think it ain't Bubbles?" Her retort had been quick, followed by a mischievous smile.

"I don't know," Jay had said. "I guess I'm just not used to people being called by their real name."

"Why? Because you're not?" she had thrown back. "By the way, what is your real name? All I know is Jay."

She remembered that Jay had squirmed and looked away before answering...

"There you go woman. Earlier you said I was always changing the subject; well, I'd say you're pretty good at it yourself. Tell you what; you tell me your real name and I'll tell you mine. Fair?"

She had explained that her real name was Barbara Jean Parramore (she had taken back her maiden name after she and Lamar had divorced) and yes, her parents had called her Bubbles from the day she was born because of her dimpled chin. When Beverly had been born with the same dimple, her dad had wanted to call her Bubbly, but her mom wouldn't stand for it.

Jay had finally relented, telling her that his name was John Roberts. "My mom started calling me Jay when I was about three, because "J" was the first letter that I learned, and I used to write it all over the backyard with a big old stick."

Bubbles remembered asking about his mom who he had mentioned twice that night.

"Oh, she was real sweet, but kind of puny as I remember. She always used to hug me a lot when I was little - before she got sick when I was in Junior High School. Then the hugging just stopped, and she took to her room where she stayed most of the time after that. 'Course, I don't guess I was too easy to love by then, anyway. She's dead now," he had added flatly.

Jay had characteristically changed the subject when she had asked about his dad. "Not much to tell," he had said. "Hey, let's see what you packed in that cooler. You were right; I am getting hungry again."

Bubbles and Jay had formed a comfortable rapport before the evening was over, and by 3:00 A.M., when they had slowly made their way back across the field arm-in-arm, she had instinctively felt that this was a man who would do her no harm, one who she desperately wanted to know better. For all of his practiced toughness and reluctant nature, Bubbles sensed that there was a confused little boy inside begging to be loved and accepted. After all, she hadn't worked as a cocktail waitress for six years without learning a thing or two about human nature.

She smiled now as she watched Jay and Jody washing off the wagon with the water hose. The sounds of laughter indicated to Bubbles that they were probably getting as much water on themselves as on the little wagon. From the first morning that they met, the two had become instant friends. Jody insisted on calling him Uncle Jay, and Jay, in turn, called her son Little Buddy. Whenever Bubbles watched them playing ball in the back yard or catching lightning bugs, she would offer a prayer of thanks for this delightful male influence in her son's life, however temporary it might be.

One of the things that Jay had taught Jody was a game called "doodle-bug,"a game with which she was unfamiliar. Peeking out of the window one day, she had watched with amusement as Jody took a thin twig, put it into a small hole in the ground, and turned it around over and over. He and Jay had carefully watched the opening of the hole as they chanted, "Doodle-bug, doodle-bug you better come out, you better come out 'cause your house is on fire." After several minutes of coaxing the alleged doodle-bug to no avail, they would cover the hole's opening with sand and leaves and move on to another spot.

"Those stupid little bugs don't know what's good for them, do they?" Jody had said.

"Nope, I reckon not, Little Buddy," Jay had answered. "They need to learn a few lessons about life. Now if you listen real good, I'll tell you a secret that those silly doodle-bugs don't know...Don't you be like them, hidin' away in dark places and doing nothin' with your life when you could be out in the light doing lots of good things. And if somebody gives you a chance to do something with your life, you grab it and make the most of it. If it looks like nobody's giving you a chance, then you find some new friends real fast."

Tears had welled up in Bubbles' eyes, and she had made a vow to learn more about this unusual man who had come into their lives.

Jay and Beverly were quite another story. Bubbles had thought that they would also become fast friends, when Bev had agreed to cut and shape Jay's long dark hair a few days after he moved in. When he had asked her to also dye it blonde, she had tried to reason with him.

"Man, that thick dark stuff of yours would probably come out all brassy looking, maybe even orangy, and you would have to touch up the color about every few weeks. You sure you want to do that?"

Jay had been adamant however, saying that his normal hair color was a light-brown anyway, and he wanted a complete new look, as he was planning to go job-hunting the following week. Beverly had consented, sending Bubbles to the drug store to buy the dye. Jay had put in an extra request for a pair of wire-rimmed reading glasses, the mildest strength, saying that he really could use a little help when he was trying to read those job applications. He promised to pay them back as soon as he got his first pay check, and he did. Bubbles remembered that he had paid them with cash, saying that he didn't fool with checking accounts. "Why should I let the banks hold on to my money when I can do that for myself?" he had said.

Jay and Bev were generally civil and polite enough to each other in Bubbles' presence, but on more than one occasion she had caught them deep in serious, sometimes rather heated conversation. Once when she asked what was going on, Bev had looked sheepishly at Jay and said, "You tell her, Jay." He had glared at her before turning to Bubbles and smiling. "Woman, can't anyone get away with anything around here? Bev and I wanted to surprise you, but it looks like we'll just have to tell you now. We want to take you and Jody this weekend to Cap'n Adam's Restaurant on the Wharf over at Panama City Beach. You don't let either of us pay any rent around here, and we just want to be able to do something nice back for you. How about it? Can you get off from work Friday night?"

Chapter 26

Dishonesty is like a boomerang - about the time you think all is well, it hits you in the back of the head.

H. Jackson Brown, Sr.

The side kitchen door slammed, jarring Bubbles' thoughts once again back to the present. Jody ran over and wrapped his dirty little arms around his mom's legs.

"You got any ice cream, Ma? Me and Uncle Jay sure are starved! We walked clean to town and back, all the way to that nice Mrs. Harris's house, but she wasn't home. I met her girl name Trish though, and she's real nice, only she's not Mrs. Harris' daughter. She was —"

"Whoa, Little Buddy," Jay interrupted, patting Jody on the head. "Slow down and catch your breath for a minute. How about letting me talk to your mom while you get us some water?"

He turned to Bubbles and said, "Woman, what's for supper? It don't look like to me you got anything cookin', and since I got paid today, why don't I run up the highway to The Burger Barn and get us all some hamburgers."

Bubbles turned her back to the sink as she hid the ground beef that was thawing, covering it with a dishrag. "Why that sure would be kind of you, sir," she drawled with an exaggerated accent, fluttering her eyelashes and laughing. "But don't you try to sweet talk me into letting you take my car, now - you hear me?"

Jody was giggling at the sink as he filled up the second glass with water. "Yuck Ma! You sound like one of them crazy ladies on the TV....Uh oh...I made a mess. I got your pretty dishrag all wet... Here Ma," he said, handing Bubbles the dripping towel. "Hey look....there's a big pile of meat under it."

Bubbles smirked and said, "Jody, boy, sometimes I wish I hadn't taught you to be so smart." Turning back to Jay she said,"Yeah, okay. So Bev did have some meat starting to thaw, but I like your idea better ...in fact, why don't I go with you? Now that I'm not working on Friday nights, it would be a real treat to go out somewhere. You know, going to Cap'n Adams' spoiled me."

Beverly agreed to take care of Jody's bath while Jay and Bubbles went to get supper.

"*Kind of like a real date,*" Bubbles thought. "*Just the two of us, and the gentleman's treating. I think I'll even let him drive.*"

Jay and Bubbles took the long way to Burger Barn, stopping along the highway by the bay, where they got out and walked down to the water. Jay expertly skimmed a few pieces of smooth shell across the calm water. The tide was out, and the protected water in this section of the bay was as smooth as glass.

"When I was a kid, I used to be able to make pebbles bounce seven or eight times across Cooter's pond. It was down the street from our trailer park. Heck, these old shell pieces don't work so good. I guess they're too ragged."

Seizing the moment, Bubbles prodded a little. "Did your dad teach you to do that, Jay?"

Jay hesitated, staring out across the water with a faraway look. "Nah," he finally said. "My old man wasn't around much, and I sure didn't learn anything good from him when he was. Most anything I know, I learned on my own, and usually the hard way."

Bubbles held her breath as he seemed inclined to continue. "Mrs. Harris, you know, was my English teacher in high school. She was one of the only people who ever complimented me and made me think that I could maybe do something right. She always said I was real smart, and she used to tell me that God loved me and so did she." Looking at Bubbles, he added, "Hey, I never believed that junk until you took me to that first revival thing that night. I kind of felt like maybe there was a God somewhere, but I sure didn't know Him. Then you made me go those next few weeks, and I think I really started paying attention to what those preachers were saying about God loving people like me who were so bad."

He ran his fingers through his short, closely cropped blonde hair. "Anyway Bubbles, ever since then, all of these good things have been happening. You probably don't know this, but I went to see Mrs. Harris one night after that first revival meeting. It was that day that you and Jody saw her at the drug store and I talked you into letting Jody call her that night. Well, I got on the phone and told her who I was and that I sure did need to see her 'cause I was having some problems. She told me to come on to her house in an hour and meet her out in the back yard by her garden shed. Remember I told you I had to go visit a friend that night? Anyway, when I got there, she hugged me just like I was still one of her students before all that - well, never mind.

We talked for quite a while, and she told me to start journalin'...writing down everything that's been going on in my life for the last few years up until now, and then just keep writing in it everyday. So, I've been doing it, and the biggest problem I've had is being real truthful. The truth sort of slaps you in the face when you see it in black and white. I've been having a hard time wonderin' how God - or anybody - could forgive me, and especially love me after some of the things I've done.

"Anyway, that's what me and Jody were taking to Mrs. Harris ... some of the things out of my journal that she had asked to read. But she wasn't there, and that girl started asking too many questions, so we left."

"Questions about what, Jay?" Bubbles asked, hoping that whatever spell had loosened his tongue would hang on a little longer.

"Aw, nothing. It's not important. Anyway, I'm starving; come on, let's go eat."

Bubbles sighed, knowing that, for now, she would have to be satisfied with this small glimpse into this complicated man's mind. However, it was a beginning, even though they had a long way to go.

There was still so much about him that she didn't know. Why was he in their little village? Where did he come from? What was he running from? What demons were haunting him, and most frustrating of all, why had he shown no more interest in her than an occasional, friendly good-night kiss revealed?

On impulse, Bubbles grabbed Jay's arm and said, "Hold on, mister. Turn around and quit running for just a minute. Come on over here and sit on this log with me, and I'll rub your shoulders. We don't have to talk or anything; you can just let go and relax for once in your life."

Two hours later, Bubbles and Jay returned to a grim-faced Beverly and a bouncy Jody who was clean and snug in his cowboy pajamas.

"Look what I found Uncle Jay. I was cleaning out my old bird cage 'cause Aunt Bev's gonna get me a new bird for my birthday...and guess what...I found this old newspaper with bird dooky all over your picture! See? It's a picture of you the way you used to look when you first came to live with us. You must be famous or something, Uncle Jay! What does it say about you?"

Beverly shot Jay an "I told you so" look, as she watched his face go pale.

"Let me see that!" Bubbles said sharply, as she snatched the paper from Jody's hands.

"Read it to me Ma," the child begged. "Aunt Bev had a real bad headache and couldn't read it. She said that I would have to wait until you and Uncle Jay got home. What took y'all so long, anyway, huh?"

Bubbles glanced at the headline and date on the newspaper, desperately hoping that there was a mistake. How could she have missed this? And what did Bev know about it? Was this why she and Jay had been so secretive at times?

The surge of blood rushing through her ears was her first clue that she was going to faint. She tried to take a deep breath, but her heart seemed to be in the way, caught somewhere up in her throat. The last thing she heard was Jody yelling, "Quick, Uncle Jay. My mom's falling; catch her!"

Bubbles regained consciousness in her own bed, gagging at the smell of household ammonia in her face. She pushed at the large hand which was waving the smelly cloth under her nose, and focused her eyes on possibly the most tormented face she had ever seen.

"Hey woman; you okay?"

Bubbles squeezed her eyes shut, willing the moment to go away. If she could just turn the clock back a few hours, back to that person who she had actually been feeling sorry for, had even dared to trust a little.

"Come on, Bubbles," the deep voice continued. "You can't shut me out forever. You might as well listen to what I have to say. I figure I owe you a lot, and I'm going to start with an explanation - a truthful one, I promise. Then if you want me to leave, I will."

Bubbles opened her eyes again, this time wiping tears from the corners. Her anger erupted with a surprising force, and she sat up, pushing her forefinger into Jay's chest.

"You're darn right! You owe me more than an explanation, Buster. You owe me an apology for starters. I don't take kindly to **nobody** moving into my home, taking advantage of my generosity, and playing around with my feelings. And when I'm finished with you, you're going to figure out what to tell that little boy in there who loves you better than Barney...and it had better be good, Mr. Robert Sloane, alias J.R., alias Jay, or whatever the crud your real name is."

Chapter 27

Hospitality is the art of making your guests feel at home, especially when you wish some of them were!

Source Unknown

The evening was much more festive out on the island at Matt's house. As she added the finishing touches, Libbie stepped back and admired the adornments on the glass top, pedestal table in the dining area. The colorful centerpiece had been sent by Jean at *Bouquets By The Bay* and featured a variety of fall flowers interspersed with seashells. The food trays were overflowing, offering shrimp molds, raw vegetables with dip, assorted fruits and cheeses, chicken fingers, and deli roast beef and ham, with accompanying dinner rolls. Dessert delicacies included pick-up lemon squares (Aunt Emma's contribution) and fudge brownies, which were proving to be a tremendous temptation to Matt. Libbie had shooed him away from the table several times already.

Matt's home was lovely, despite the sparse furnishings of a single man who was attempting to start over. Upon entering, one was treated to a picturesque view of the Gulf of Mexico, seen through the floor-to-ceiling plate-glass windows which enclosed three sides of the massive great room. The walls rose to a height of twenty-four feet, where they met a pickled, oak-beamed ceiling. The two upstairs bedrooms opened off of a balcony which overlooked the great room. On the angled fourth wall of the great room was a massive stone fireplace which served not only the living area, but also the dining area which opened off to the left.

The foyer, kitchen, dining area, and bathrooms were all smartly floored in Mexican tile, which was not only easy to keep clean, but added a beachy charm. The great room, halls, and bedrooms had blonde, hardwood floors, and Matt's only accessory splurge so far had been the purchase of a lovely, colorful Dhurrie rug for the great room.

Several guests had arrived early, among them Sam and Annie Penton. They found Libbie and Matt out on the large wooden deck, sipping lemonade and nibbling on chips and dip.

"Hey, somebody told me there was a party here," Sam announced in his booming voice when he walked out on the deck. Stopping to grab a hand full of chips and survey the view, Sam continued, "Matt, old boy, you've done yourself real proud here. I should have gone into preaching instead of the newspaper business. Looks like it pays a whole lot better."

Matt hopped out of the wooden swing to shake Sam's hand, but not before the reporter's eagle eye noticed how close the reverend and Libbie had been sitting.

"Hey Sam and Annie," Matt said. "Welcome to my humble home which, I can assure you, will take a lot of years of preaching and praying too before it's really mine. You two come join us; we were just enjoying one of the most beautiful sunsets I've ever seen. Grab something to drink and pull up a chair."

"I believe I will," Sam replied. "But I'll pass on the lemonade, thanks. It's one of the few typically southern things that I haven't cultivated a taste for. I go for the hard stuff, you know, the leaded stuff." He pulled a canned cola out of a large ice chest and turned to his wife. "Annie, what can I get for you?"

"Nothing thanks, Honey," Annie replied. "You all enjoy the sunset; I think I'll go in and chat with Mrs. Harris for a few minutes." She turned and stepped inside, only to stick her head back out the door, giggling. "Hey guys," she called, "Mildred is coming in the front door with Soloman and Ella in tow, and it looks like she's bending their ear about something. I really admire you, Matt. I don't know how you keep your cool when she comes in over at the church trying to run things like she does."

Matt smiled. "Patience is a virtue that I constantly strive to cultivate, Annie. Actually, the Lord and I have worked hard to channel the well-meaning efforts of 'certain' church members into constructive avenues, and we have discovered that Mildred is a wonderful receptionist and phone chairman - oops, excuse me, 'chairperson.'" He winked at Annie. "Remind me to tell you about her first experience with the caller return. If the good Lord didn't have a sense of humor, it would have tried even His patience." He moved toward the deck door to open it for Annie who graciously stepped aside to let the newcomers out.

"Evening Mildred," Matt said to the voluptuous, middle-aged woman dressed in a mammoth, brightly-colored, flowered shift, which called extra attention to her already imposing self. "I see you've brought Soloman and Ella with you. Glad you folks could come."

Matt always welcomed Soloman Horton's firm handshake. The large, well-built gentleman was unusually strong for someone in his late fifties. However, his gentle demeanor, one of his most endearing qualities, was in sharp contrast to his physical appearance. His deep, rich voice was melodic, developed from years of singing in the church choir as well as in revivals and community sings. He would be a hard person to compete against in the story-telling contest, his mellow, hypnotic deliverance of the ghost story sure to captivate any audience.

"Well, big man; it's about time that you and your lovely wife paid me a visit," Matt said to Soloman. "Just because you folks are good Baptists doesn't mean you can't bring those grandchildren out sometime to swim at the Congregational Minister's house. You know Brother Roy from your church visited just last week. He is seriously considering buying the empty lot next to mine. Don't you think we could have some terrific combined church parties here on the beach?

"Hey Soloman," he continued. "I'm real anxious to hear your campaign slogan tonight. I'm warning all of you guys that you've got some pretty stiff competition with Mrs. Harris. You know she's already jumped the gun, so to speak - put a few of her signs out last week."

"Yeah, that's what I've heard," Soloman responded with a big grin. "Peers to me like maybe she's runnin' a little bit scared of ol' Soloman here. Shoot, everybody knows there ain't no story around that can top my story about Cap'n Pete and the Moss Lady. Yes sir, my daddy pop used to tell us grandchildren about the Cap'n sometimes when we was all spendin' the night with him and Mud-dear. I'm here to tell you we'd be so scared that, by the time he was finished, all seven of us would be huddled together under one blanket as far away from the front door of their old house as we could get. Daddy Pop, he'd just laugh and say we looked like a batch of newborn puppies all tangled up and wet behind the ears. Then Mud-dear would offer us hot chocolate, and the older ones would jump out first, sayin' they was just under that ol' blanket to keep the rest of us young'ns from being too upset. Shoot, we never did hear that story that we didn't get plumb scared to death! But don't you worry none, Reverend; I aim to tone it down when I tell it, so the little children won't be too spooked."

Turning to Ella, Matt winked and said, "Miss Ella, I'm counting on you to keep him under control. They say behind every good man there's a good woman, and I know he's in good hands with you helping him."

Ella Horton faked a demure smile which lit up the most unusual, sensational, golden-brown eyes that Matt had ever seen. "Oh go on with you, Reverend. Don't you see me blushing now," she joked.

Others trickled in slowly, and Jimbo and Shelley, characteristically, were the last to come, their arrival announced by the smooth roar of his diesel truck. For the next hour everyone enjoyed the food, ocean breezes and informal tours of Matt's new home.

Mildred took the opportunity to offer several bits of advice on window treatments, for which Matt kindly thanked and ignored her at the same time. Libbie smiled at his diplomatic patronization of the obnoxious, but well-meaning lady, intrigued, yet again, by another side of this seemingly predictable, but in reality, complex man of many talents. "*Smooth, Matt,*" she thought, with a growing sense of fascination and admiration.

Matt was able to politely excuse himself from Mildred when Libbie suggested that it might be time to start discussing business, since it was getting late.

"OK folks," he announced from the breakfast room, next to the window that Mildred had insisted would look lovely with Belgium lace curtains. "Let's all find a seat and finalize our plans for the festival and our new event. The community is getting excited now, and they are expecting a big article in the newspaper."

Moving toward the fireplace, he continued. "I need all of the 'Big Mouths' up front by the hearth here, and y'all bring your campaign slogan posters. The rest of you have your committee reports ready to discuss with us."

The small group settled quickly, with an occasional straggler reluctant to leave the food table. Mildred and Libbie had decided to put away some of the perishables and clean the kitchen, until Matt called them back.

"That can wait, ladies. We need your input here, too. Come on and join us," he called, pulling two chairs up next to where he was standing.

"Now the first thing I think we need to decide is where we would like to donate the money raised by these big mouths here. I know the other festival donations pretty much follow the same agenda each year, and they have all proven to be worthy causes that count on our proceeds. I would like to suggest that we pick something new for the 'Big Mouths' to sponsor. But that's just my opinion. Let's hear what some of you think."

Little discussion was needed for the group to reach a unanimous consensus; the money raised from the "Big Mouth" campaign would go to support the new rehabilitation wing of the hospital. The hospital was already planning to have a large Open House announcement in the paper the following week, with information on personnel to be hired and services to be offered. Sam promised to co-ordinate the two announcements with side-by-side articles on the front page of The Village Voice.

The contestants thrilled the group with their campaign posters and slogans, and the suggestion was made that the new contest might renew an enthusiasm and excitement in their community that had been cautiously hidden since the tornado and rash of crimes throughout the spring and summer.

Everyone, of course, already knew Mrs. Harris' slogan about spinning a yarn, but she delighted them all with a display of her grandmotherly poster. With a twinkle in his eye, Big Soloman Horton acknowledged that her poster was indeed lovely, but he assured her that she would have to "run hard" to catch up with him. He then held up his poster which brought "aahs" and claps from the group. Soloman had gone out to his friend Oscar's farm and had his picture taken next to one big, mean, old bull. He was facing the bull and had his hands cupped around his mouth as if he was yelling into the bull's ear. The caption stated, "Big Soloman can tell a big tale, and that's no bull!"

Next, Sam, who had the benefit of photography tricks not available to most people, showed his poster which featured an enlarged picture of his wide-open mouth, superimposed on a smaller version of his face. The background was a map of the southern part of the United States below the Mason-Dixon Line. The caption stated, "Vote for Sam Penton, the Yankee mouth of the south!" Everyone loved the idea, but Mildred wanted to know why his eyes were looking toward the west instead of the south.

Last, as usual, was Jimbo, patiently awaiting his turn with a relaxed smile. "Y'all sure are smart with all of them fancy words and pictures. Heck, I'm just a plain old country boy, and I reckon that's why the people are gonna love me the best," he said, as he held up a picture of himself standing next to a huge, prize-winning marlin which was hanging from hooks at the dock. The caption read, "Catch Jimbo Hopkin's story; it's sure to be a whopper!"

Around 10:30, Matt walked Libbie and Emmaline to their car. They all agreed that the party had been a huge success, and they were eager to officially begin the Big Mouth Campaign.

After putting Emmaline's trays and Libbie's ice bucket on the back seat of the Honda, Matt turned to the two ladies. Extending both arms out, he drew Libbie and Emmaline into a giant bear hug.

"Ladies, I would like to thank you two for the support and encouragement that you have given me since I moved to Apalachicola. It's been a long time since I have felt so happy and fulfilled, and I count each of you as a special blessing."

He leaned his six-foot, two-inch frame over, out of necessity, to kiss the little five-foot gray-haired lady on the cheek. When he straightened up and turned to Libbie - who was not much taller than her aunt - he was momentarily distracted by her smile and the sparkle in her deep, aqua-green eyes. Her loose blonde curls were blowing softly in the ocean breeze, and Matt again felt a longing that he had tried to neatly pack away years ago. He gently brushed her lips with his, catching a light whiff of perfume. The catch in his throat stifled his attempt to murmur "thanks," and the only word that escaped his mouth was "Libbie."

Chapter 28

Who, being loved, is poor?
  Oscar Wilde

Jimmy Johns waved at the big, yellow school bus as it lumbered by. The morning was crisp and bright, and Jimmy stretched his arms skyward as he took in a deep breath of the fresh air. He retrieved the Monday morning edition of *The Village Voice* from the curb and headed back toward the front door of his trailer.

"I sure wisht my ma would get out on a pretty day like this," he thought. *"I bet her lungs would go on and clear up if she breathed somethin' besides that ol' cigarette smoke. She keeps sayin' her ol' legs won't carry her, but I can't see what that has to do with them cigarettes."*

He left the front door open and turned on the ceiling fan in the little living room. Then he went into the kitchen and opened the window over the sink. The air conditioner was on the blink, and he knew that the little trailer would be steamy by 11:00, but he could enjoy the nice morning air at least for a little while before he had to leave for the church.

Jimmy poured himself a glass of milk and sat down at the faded green Formica kitchen table to look at the newspaper. He would look at the pictures like he always did, read what he could, and then take the paper back to his mother's bedroom, along with her cup of coffee.

Jimmy's face lit up with a wide grin as he unfolded the paper and saw the pictures of his friends. "Ma, come on up here and just look at this, will ya? I've got a big surprise for ya. Come on, ma; it's a really nice mornin' and you're not gonna believe who all's on the front page today."

Jimmy listened hopefully as he heard the springs squeak in Virginia Johns' bed down the hall. Maybe she would get out of bed today before he left. He always hated to leave her back there in that hot room with the windows closed.

"Hey listen, Ma. Here's Ms. Harris with a hat on - kinda like the one you used to wear when you worked in the garden. And Mr. Soloman's here standin' next to a big ol' bull. He looks like he's whisperin' in his ear or somethin'." Jimmy peeked around the corner but saw no sign of his mother in the hall.

"Ma, are ya' comin'? You've gotta see this, really. You've never seen Mr. Sam with such a big mouth. And here's Mr. Jimbo. Man is that a big fish he's standin next to. I can't figure out what they're all doin' but it....." Jimmy looked up into the drawn face of his frail little mother and smiled big enough for both of them.

"Here, sit down Ma. I'll get ya' some coffee, and you can read to me all about what my friends are doing in the paper."

Ginger Johns sipped her coffee slowly as she quickly scanned the headlines. She grieved for her only son, so eager and full of life, and yet so incapable of enjoying it to the fullest. Her physical handicaps were certainly limiting, but thank goodness she had a keen mind and could always immerse herself in a good book, temporarily escaping the reality of her tormented existence. Poor Jimmy couldn't even read the titles of most of the books that he so kindly brought home to her from the library.

She started to pull out a cigarette from her robe pocket, but thought better of it, knowing how much it bothered Jimmy. Instead, she reached for the little bottle of capsules that Jimmy's friend, Mrs. Harris, had sent to her. She felt bad that she hadn't taken them daily like Jimmy had said she was supposed to. After she had tried them for a few days and hadn't been able to tell any difference, she had pushed them behind the toaster and forgotten them. But for some reason this morning, it was important that she make Jimmy happy. His extraordinary enthusiasm today was almost contagious.

"Well, son, it says here that your friends are all in a contest. They're gonna see who can tell the best story at the Seafood Festival, and they're askin' their friends to vote for who they think is the best storyteller."

Ginger noticed a frown on her son's face and wondered what she had said to cause such a look.

"Gosh, Ma, I don't think I could pick one of my friends over the other one. What should I do?"

Ginger patted his hand softly and said, "Honey, you just tell all of them that you think they're wonderful and don't worry none about it."

Long after Jimmy was gone, Ginger remained in the front room of the trailer, actually enjoying the morning breeze from the open front door. She made a mental note to get Jimmy to buy some screen to replace the large torn upper portion of the screened door. Maybe the nice weather today was a sign of an early fall.

Ginger picked up the paper again, unable to get the other front-page article out of her mind, the one about the new rehabilitation center at the hospital. It said that they would be able to help people with all kinds of crippling diseases.... and it also gave a description of the jobs that would be available. One of the positions listed was receptionist, and the smallest glimmer of interest stirred within Ginger.

Years ago, before Jimmy's birth, Virginia Johns had been a receptionist at the mill. She had been a valuable asset to the company, and during her difficult pregnancy, they had been very supportive and accommodating. However, a rapid rise in her blood pressure had forced her to quit, and shortly after Jimmy was born, she had suffered what the doctors believed to be a stroke. Since that time, she had been an invalid with limited use of her legs. She had not tried to work again, knowing that her son needed her more than they needed the money. Lately, however, it seemed that she had become more dependent on Jimmy than he was on her.

Could this new facility possibly help her walk better? Probably not, on her small disability income; she was sure that this new fancy place would be real expensive. She briefly allowed herself to wonder if they would consider someone like her for a front-desk position. Just as quickly, she answered her own question. Heck, she didn't even have a nice dress anymore, let alone know how to put on make-up or fix her hair. And she hadn't been out in public in so long, that she wasn't sure she would even know how to talk to folks. Besides, she knew they wouldn't let her smoke in a hospital place like that, so she was just wasting her time even thinking about it.

Virginia Johns crumbled up the newspaper and stuffed it in the overflowing trash can. She lit a cigarette and slowly hobbled back down the hall.

A few miles down the highway, Beverly Parramore poured her second cup of coffee and unplugged the pot. Now that Jody was in school, she more or less had the house to herself in the early mornings. On very few occasions, Bubbles would sleep in if her night shift the previous evening had been unusually late. But generally she got up in time to take Jay to work, then drop Jody off at school before running errands. She would usually manage to catch up on lost sleep from around 10:00 until 3:00, skipping lunch in the process.

Bev ambled into the living room, picked up the Monday morning paper where Jay had left it and turned on the Today show. The news was on, filled with the latest allegations about the sex scandal in Washington. Beverly clicked the remote to mute, sick of hearing about the President's personal problems, when she and her family had enough problems of their own. Thank goodness sex wasn't one of them at the moment!

Her thoughts drifted back to the previous Friday night, when a controversy rivaling the emotions of the White House scandals had erupted in their own little modest home. She remembered the scared look on Jody's pale little face when his mother had fainted. When Jay had carried Bubbles to her room, he had explained to Jody that his mother just needed some rest and would be better in the morning.

It had been Bev's job to comfort and re-assure her nephew that evening, trying to explain to him why he couldn't go in to see his mom when she, Beverly, was having such a hard time with the situation herself. She had finally calmed the little fellow, given him a forbidden bedtime bowl of ice cream, and snuggled with him in his twin bed, rubbing his back until he dropped off to sleep.

Afterwards, Beverly had fallen into a restless sleep on the living room sofa, waiting anxiously for someone to emerge from behind the closed door of Bubbles' room. Her dreams had been troubled, fueled in part by her anxiety over the deathly silence from the bedroom. Was Bubbles all right? How much was Jay telling her? Would Bubbles ever forgive her for not telling what she had known for months? Would she understand that they had simply been trying to protect Bubbles and Jody by not telling?

Around 3:00 A. M. a penitent-looking Jay had opened the bedroom door and walked toward the kitchen. Instantly awakened, Beverly had sat up, looking around cautiously. On his way back through the living room with a glass of water in his hand, Jay had whispered to Bev that Bubbles would like to talk to her.

As Beverly thought back over the evening's conversation, she was still overwhelmed with the memory of her sister's powerful love, understanding, forgiveness, and determination. No one that she knew but Bubbles could find hope in such a frightening and confusing set of circumstances, and Beverly knew that only her sister's faith provided her with such strength. Even more overwhelming was the fact that for the first time in years, Beverly had felt the powerful presence of Bubbles' loving God in that little bedroom when her sister had asked that they all hold hands and pray.

Reveling now in her thoughts, Beverly took a deep breath and experimented with her own little prayer, something that she had not attempted in a long time.

"Well, good morning, Sir; it's me, Beverly. Remember, I used to talk to you a lot when I was a little girl with that polio? Then, you know, I sort of got mad at you when I didn't heal up completely, and I thought that was why my daddy left us and all. So, anyway, in case you don't know, I've just been trying to handle things on my own since then. Of course, you probably know that too, don't you?

"Bubbles says you know everything, even before it happens. Well sir, I don't mind telling you that's kind of scary to me. But Bubbles, she says we ought to be thankful for that, because wherever we go, you will already be there ahead of us taking care of business. And she says that you won't never let anything happen to us so bad that we can't handle it if we let you help us...Is that so, sir?

"And, since I'm talking to you and all like this, I'm just wondering how you're supposed to answer me. You know, I have to be honest with you again, sir, and tell you that it will probably scare me to death if all of a sudden I hear some deep, booming voice coming out of the sky. You don't do that anymore, do you? Seems like I remember from Sunday School that you did that kind of stuff in the Old Testament days? I'm real sorry, sir, but I don't know too much about the Bible... But then you know that too don't you?

"Whoa, now I'm getting a little psyched! If you know so much, then you know all the bad stuff about me. Maybe this was a mistake; I guess I've probably already ruined my chances by now. But, sir, I really have tried most of the time to be good and all. Even Jay seems to think that you're helping him now, and I know I've never been as bad as him.

"Oh well, I wouldn't even feel right asking you for any help since I ain't done much for you in my lifetime. Besides, my list would be so long, neither one of us would know where to start - begging your pardon, sir, because Bubbles says you know everything. But, I will tell you that I do feel better since we had this little talk, even if I've been doing all the talking. So, if you ever feel it in your heart to answer me back somehow, I sure would appreciate it, sir. Just make sure that I know it's you."

Beverly opened her eyes, curled her legs up, and unfolded the newspaper in her lap. The headlines read, "New Rehabilitation Clinic to Open." The first paragraph stated that the clinic would offer therapy for numerous physical afflictions, specializing in rehabilitation for victims of polio. Beverly had a hard time reading the rest of the article, as her eyes were clouded with tears.....and she knew.

Chapter 29

A wise man will make more opportunities than he finds.

Francis Bacon

Everyone in the area, including East Point, Carrabelle, and St. George Island, was talking about the colorful fish faces that had suddenly appeared around the village, and rumor had it that the president himself was the mysterious celebrity lined up to attend the event. Only Jimbo and Shelley knew for sure, and they weren't talking —yet.

Anxious to be in on the action, citizens were standing in lines all over town at the designated places of business, eager to buy their $1.00 voting slips and join the fish- feeding frenzy. However, the contestants seemed to be more enthused than anybody.

Mrs. Emmaline Harris and Sam Penton (with help from Annie) were passing out homemade goodies on the downtown sidewalks and in the stores. Big Soloman was entertaining passers-by on the main street corner of town, wearing his top hat and singing New Orleans style folk songs with his banjo for accompaniment, and Jimbo Hopkins was offering free sunset cruises up the river.

The town's merchants were thrilled with the increase in business. Mr. Jones at the hardware store was even offering a free voting slip with each $20.00 purchase. And of course Velma - not one to be outdone - offered a free voting ticket plus a shampoo and set to the first ten customers who bought her new Lady Boutique Facial Kits.

The enthusiasm in the village sparked a new level of interest in the town's appearance. Even though they had modernized and spruced up after the tornado, the citizens felt that the possibility of a visit from the president himself surely justified extra effort. After all, there would probably be television cameras and crews from all of the major networks, and it just wouldn't do for one of them to trip over Mr. Jones' old hound who slept all day on the sidewalk in front of his store. Or even worse, what if the president's car hit one of those huge potholes left by the tornado and suffered a blow-out.

The Town Council met on Monday evening a week after the fish faces were put out. Jimbo and Shelley had promised the council that they would reveal the name of the mysterious celebrity as soon as they had a confirmation. However, the consensus of the representatives was that no matter who the visitor might be, or if there even was one, several improvements were long overdue.

Those pot holes on Main Street would be repaired immediately, and if there was time, the whole street would be re-paved and striped. Any bent, broken, or faded street signs would either be replaced or repainted, depending on the severity of the need. And artificial flowers would be removed from the cement pots on the street corners downtown. In their place would be live, colorful pansies with fresh ivy surrounding the flowers and cascading down the sides of the planters.

The garbage cans on the sidewalks would be enclosed in beadboard framed boxes painted to match the nearby store fronts, and those broken concrete steps along one block of Main Street would finally be repaired. One member commented that the steps should have been taken care of after the tornado.

"Well, Joe," the chairman replied, "it seems like they've just always been that way. I don't reckon we ever thought much about it before now."

The cheerleaders from the local high school got involved, sponsoring a car wash the following Saturday and raising enough money to buy a new flag for the court house. They even made up a new cheer in anticipation of the president coming, and they were delighted to share it with their customers....

> "Mr. President, you're our man,
> if you can't do it, nobody can...
> We've looked near, and we've looked far,
> but none come close - you're still our star!"

By the end of the second week, the fish faces had spit out a collective total of 2,318 ballots, translating to $2,318.00. With four weeks left until the festival, plus the big culminating event to be held on the night of the storytelling, the excitement was reaching euphoria. In addition, competition was enhanced by the announcement that Mrs. Emmaline Harris was the present front runner.

Chapter 30

What matters is not the size of the dog in the fight, but the size of the fight in the dog.
                          Coach Bear Bryant

Velma hadn't slept well Friday night. She kept thinking that she heard noises next door at the beauty parlor. Around 4:00 A.M. she even thought that she saw a small light flicker inside the building, but then it had gone out, and things had seemed quiet again. She had considered waking Billy up, but he had fussed so much lately about her overreacting to everything, that she had decided against it.

At 4:30, she gave up trying to sleep. She had a big day ahead of her, and she decided that she might as well get up and get started. Besides her three regulars, she had four people coming in to buy her Lady Boutique kits and get their free shampoo and set. *"Oh,"* she thought, *"If only that Beverly would come back. That new girl I hired this week ain't worth grits."*

Even though Billy was sleeping in the next room, Velma dressed quietly in the dark, unwilling to be blinded this early in the morning by the overhead light. When she got to the shop, she would brush her teeth and use her Lady Boutique facial and make-up kit. She would make some coffee and toast in the shop's little kitchen while she unpacked the twenty large boxes of Lady Boutique supplies that U.P.S. had brought late Friday afternoon.

Velma crept out of her front door around 4:45 A.M. in the cool, quiet dark of early morning. The sliver of moon sinking on the horizon shed little light as she made her way across the front yard and through the well-used gap in the ligustrum hedge. On the other side of the hedge, the yard of the beauty salon was draped in shadows from a giant Magnolia tree. Billy had wanted to cut it down years ago, but Velma had stood firm. The soft, sweet scent of the Magnolia blossoms tickled her nose, and once again she was glad that she had not given in to one of Billy's tirades.

As she neared the rock garden by the front steps, she suddenly stopped in dismay and turned her small flashlight beam toward the flamingo grouping. Sure enough, the lead flamingo was facing toward her house, the opposite direction from the six others. She was sure that he had been facing the right way when she closed the shop last night. In fact, she had made a point lately to check her little birds when she left each evening, after all of the trouble that she had been having with them.

"I'm just plumb sick and tired of this," she grumbled while turning the wayward fellow back around. "I wonder if somebody's playing a stupid joke on me, or what. It's probably just a bunch of kids, so I ain't gonna get too worked up about it. But I know it sure does get Billy all upset if I try to fix it back. Well, this time he won't even have to know.

"Thank goodness he's about to leave for a week on the road. Maybe I'll get a little peace and quiet around here," she thought. "Sometimes I wish he'd go on and take one of them cruises he keeps getting brochures about in the mail; I could really get some rest then."

Velma's key slipped easily into the lock, and she automatically reached for the light switch inside the door to the right. As she stepped inside, a noise in the back of the shop caused her to freeze. It was too loud to be one of those mouse traps that she had recently set, and after the noises that she had heard last night, she wasn't taking any chances.

As a precaution, she left the front door open and slowly edged toward her desk where she kept a mace stun gun. She had bought it back during the summer when all of those robberies had been going on. Just as she reached for the drawer she heard footprints, then heard the back door of the shop slam.

Velma grabbed her mace gun and ran back out of the front door. She wasn't sure what to do next, and her heart was beating so wildly that she had to stop for a minute just to catch her breath. However, she didn't get to rest for long before she heard a strange squeaking noise and what sounded like someone running across the backyard. She flattened herself up against the wall of the front porch and peeked around the corner of the house just in time to see a figure in dark clothing pushing what appeared to be a shopping cart full of boxes. He was headed toward a small gray truck parked along the curb of the empty lot behind her house.

After turning on every light in the front of the shop, Velma grabbed the phone and dialed 911. On the third ring a sleepy female voice drawled, "This is 911. May I help you?"

"Yes, yes, hurry - call the police! I've just been robbed."

Slightly more alert, the operator asked, "Ma'am, are you okay?"

"Yes, I'm fine, but the person just left my shop and someone needs to try and catch him."

"Calm down, now, ma'am." the voice instructed. "Tell me, are you alone?"

"Yes, but I've got my stun gun with me."

"Okay, ma'am, was there more than one person?"

Velma was ready to explode. This dingbat on the other end of the line was wasting valuable time and they were getting nowhere.

"How should I know?" she yelled. "I only saw one, and I'm not stupid enough to go back there to check for more. That's why I called you people!"

"Hold on, please," the monotone voice said, and Velma was sure that she watched the sun rise while she waited.

Finally the person came back and instructed Velma to stay on the line with her until the police arrived.

"How can you send them when you don't even know where I am?" Velma asked impatiently.

"I've got your address on my screen and I've dispatched them from another phone," the voice replied evenly. Velma had to grudgingly admit that maybe this annoyingly calm, collected person really did know what she was doing after all...

Billy was furious! After the police left he slammed the rear door of the shop and kicked a pile of empty boxes, scattering them all over the back storage room.

"I thought you was going to empty all of them boxes last night," he yelled. "And what the devil did you call the police for? Now you've gone and made a big deal out of nothing again."

"Excuse me, but I don't think my walking in on a robbery is nothing, Billy. I could have been killed!" she cried.

"Yeah, well you weren't, were you? You weren't even threatened. And it looks like to me you weren't even robbed. Least that's what the police come up with."

"Maybe not, but they dumped all of my new Lady Boutique kits all over the floor and took most of my boxes. And anyway, what's it to you when I unpack my stuff? It *is* my business, you know...thanks to my dear dad's money, God rest his soul. So I can do what I want with my inventory, you hear me?"

Velma started picking through the pieces of broken bottles, trying to salvage as much as possible. "It just don't make any sense," she grumbled. "What could they have been after, for goodness sakes, and anyway, how did they get in? There's no sign of a forced entry."

"Who cares, Velma," Billy scoffed as he picked up the remaining Lady Boutique box and poured its contents onto the floor with the rest of the kits' remains. "It's for sure they didn't want none of this junk."

Velma stood up and put her hands on her hips. "Billy Jernigan, if you're not gonna help me clean up this mess, then get on out of here," she yelled. "I've had about all I can take for one morning without you......."

"Excuse me, but what seems to be the problem, Mrs. Jernigan?" a smooth cultivated voice inquired from the door to the next room.

Velma looked into the cool, blue eyes of a stranger whose slightly lined faced appeared to be that of a man in his early sixties. His thinning, Grecian Formula enhanced hair revealed an obvious vain attempt to cover what Velma suspected would naturally be striking silver gray. She prided herself on being able to spot these things pretty fast.

"Is this man bothering you?" the poised, well-dressed gentleman continued, and Velma found herself wondering what kind of match he would be for her husband if Billy characteristically took offense. Even though Billy was behind her, Velma could sense his rage almost before he opened his mouth.

"Who wants to know?" Billy fired back, then spit on Velma's floor.

The older man stepped to the side and was joined by a tanned, well-built younger man dressed in jeans, a Hard Rock Cafe T-shirt and a Seafood Festival baseball cap.

"My nephew and I would like to know, sir. We have just brought my wife, Mrs. Morgan, for her Saturday morning hair appointment with Mrs. Jernigan, but we're inclined not to leave her, considering the circumstances. Maybe you'd like to explain to us why the police just left, and while you're explaining, I'd like to know your reasons for treating this lovely lady here with such little respect."

Billy's face registered a look of surprise at the appearance of the nephew, then he quickly looked away. He strolled over to Velma and put his arm around her waist. She tried to wiggle free, but his hold was strong, and the fingers from his tight grip were digging into the flesh at her waist.

"Well, for your information, hot shot, this here's my little lady, and I'll treat her any way I want to. But, mind you, she ain't complainin', are ya' sugar?" If possible, his fingers dug in deeper, and Velma gritted her teeth.

Ignoring Billy's question and trying to appear calm, she looked straight at the older gentleman and said, "Well, Mr. Morgan, it sure is nice to finally meet you, sir. Tell Mrs. Morgan to make herself comfortable and I'll be right with her. We had a little robbery attempt here last night, and I was just trying to clean up some before my customers arrived."

Taking advantage of Billy's slightly loosened grip, she pulled away quickly and went over to drop a broken bottle in the trash can. "Why don't you two gentlemen come have some coffee?" she said, as she exited the room with the grace of a queen, never once looking back at her scowling husband. The two men stepped aside for her, then glanced back to see Billy heading out the back door. Vance Morgan spoke to his nephew in a low voice... "Rex, why don't you have a quick look around back here. I'll get us some coffee and wait for you in the front room; don't I remember that you like yours with one sugar, like your dad did?"

At 10:00 sharp, Mrs. Emmaline Harris arrived at Velma's for her standing appointment, her arms full of campaign posters and homemade peanut butter brittle. She was dismayed to find that Sam Penton, of all people, was there in her sacred territory, and Velma, Mildred, Claire and Vince Morgan, plus a nice-looking young stranger were gathered around him.

"Well, well, look who's here," Emmaline called out when the bell over the door announced her arrival and no one but Velma even looked up. "Sam, what are you doing in Velma's beauty parlor on a Saturday morning? Surely you weren't one of the first ten to buy a Lady Boutique Facial Kit?" she teased. "Here," she continued, "Have some peanut brittle, Sam...and don't forget who gave it to you."

Sam smiled and gladly accepted her offering. "Sorry I don't have anything to offer in return, Ms. Emma, but I'm out on official business this morning. Say, why don't you drop by the house later in the morning though, around 11:30 or 12:00, and Annie ought to be pulling fresh brownies out of the oven. That includes all of you," he said to the others in the room. "Believe me, her brownies will taste a lot better while they're warm than later in the day, when I'm passing them out downtown," he said through a mouth full of peanut brittle. Licking his fingers, he said, "Oh my, Ms. Emma, this is about as good as it gets!" He gave her an affectionate hug and added, "I hope that you'll have some of this around when I win the contest...You remember, of course, 'to the victor go the spoils.'"

Sam turned back to Velma and, with his pencil poised over the small notebook in his hand, asked if there was anything else of importance that she could remember. Sam very seldom interviewed people with a tape recorder, and never took his lap top on an interview. But he could always be seen around town with a pencil stuck behind his ear and a small writing pad in his pocket.

"No, Sam; that's about it. Like I said, he didn't really take anything that I can see but some boxes, and the weird thing is he emptied them first! He sure did mess up a bunch of my new Lady Boutique kits though, probably close to a thousand dollars worth of damage."

Emmaline Harris, careful to turn up her hearing aid, listened thoughtfully before asking, "Did you have a break-in, dear?"

"Yes ma'am, during the night," Velma answered, more relaxed now and gratified by the concern that everyone had expressed throughout the morning. "I came in on somebody early this mornin', right after I had turned that blamed flamingo back around outside. You know, Ms. Harris, seems like that flamingo was turned wrong on another Saturday morning when you was here, do you remember?"

At this point, Sam was paying little attention to the ladies' conversation. He was, however, pulling a campaign poster out of his briefcase. He remembered noticing that Ms. Emma had come in with her posters earlier.

"Velma," he interrupted, "Excuse me for interrupting, but I've got to be going so I can get this article ready for tomorrow's paper."

"Oh Sam, how can I thank you for coming over so fast? I'm thinkin' if we get the word out quick enough, somebody might remember seeing somethin' and we can catch this guy."

"Yeah, I hope you're right," Sam replied. "Say, and Velma, if you really want to thank me, why don't you let me put up one of my campaign posters in your front window here?"

Glancing over at a frowning Emmaline, he continued mischievously, "Right next to Mrs. Harris' poster, of course."

Chapter 31

*I had never seen a church like that; it was
nearly impossible to be a mere observer.*
                                        Robert Duvall

Sunday morning dawned with an overcast sky and the smell of rain threatening to dampen the spirits of the Riverside Congregational Women's Missionary Society. They had met at the church early that morning to make preparations for the afternoon dinner on the grounds which kicked off the church's annual tithe drive each fall.

"I just knew it," Mildred declared. "Don't y'all remember how the weather systems started getting all messed up after we put the first man on the moon in the sixties? My dad used to say back then that we ought to stay out of the heavens. 'That's God's territory,' he would say, 'and we shouldn't be messing with the laws of nature.'"

"So, what's your point, Mildred?" one of the ladies called out as she smoothed and carefully inspected the red-checked plastic cloths to be used on the tables outside.

"Well, think about it," Mildred answered. "The laws of nature around Apalachicola have gone haywire this year. Some people say its because of that El Niño thing, and I say it's all connected with those weird things that have been going on. It seems to me like every time something bad happens around here, the weather acts up too. Just like this weekend; don't you know Velma's place was hit Friday night, and sure enough, now our dinner on the grounds is going to get rained out," Mildred fumed, partially perturbed by the fact that the weather was one thing over which she had absolutely no control.

"Girl, you must be a sound sleeper," another member responded. "The rain came through sometime during the night, hard and heavy, but the weather report has predicted sunny skies by noon."

Sure enough, when the service let out around 11:50, thanks to Matt's considerate, short sermon - not to mention his hearty appetite - the side yard of Riverside Congregational Church looked like a picture out of *Southern Homes and Gardens*. The ladies had worked hard, and a warm sun beamed on the results of their efforts.

Picnic tables covered with the red-checked table cloths were set up at random around the freshly-mowed lawn. In the middle of each table was a basket of colorful mums. The food tables were off to the side, under a grove of pine trees which served to protect the variety of homemade dishes from the noon-day sun. Some church members were spreading quilts on the slightly damp grass, and others were setting up groups of folding lawn chairs, leaving the tables to the visitors and older members.

Matt had stressed casual attire and had encouraged his congregation to invite their friends this year in keeping with the church's new mission statement about sharing God's love in the community. The church's sign out front invited all to "Come as you are; God loves you that way." Thus, few were surprised to see Sam and Annie Penton come strolling across the yard - Sam in his jeans - pushing Virginia Johns in a wheel chair, and a grinning Jimmy walking next to them carrying a basket of cookies. Not far behind them was Brenda Coggins and her father, Bernie, the latter looking suspiciously uncomfortable as his wary eyes appeared to search the grounds for something out of the ordinary.

Mildred spotted the newcomers first and immediately rushed over to welcome them, as was only befitting her status as Social Chairperson. Matt wasn't far behind, excusing himself from Libbie and Emmaline who had just arrived after their own church service had let out.

Members and guests feasted lavishly on a variety of casseroles, vegetables, salads, jello delights, pickled relished, sliced ham, fried chicken, roast beef, rolls, corn bread, and a selection of desserts which included pies, cakes, cookies, brownies and puddings. The missionary ladies of the church, wearing matching red-checked aprons, circulated throughout the meal offering coffee, tea, and lemonade.

A slight breeze and the warm sun added a relaxed, hypnotic quality to the afternoon, and by 1:00, an occasional member could be found stretched out on a blanket with their eyes closed, some covering their faces with caps. Others were visiting around in small groups, washing down a last bite of dessert with drink refills. The teenagers and a few energetic young adults were passing footballs, and the smaller children were running around barefooted playing tag.

Matt pulled his eyes away from an animated Libbie who was describing to Virginia Johns her first visit to the rehabilitation exercise room. His gaze wandered over the faces of his congregates and friends, and his heart swelled with pure, raw joy. "Oh my God," he silently offered up. "I, among all men am most surely blessed."

Within an hour, the crowd started breaking up, as the missionary ladies cleaned up the last of the remains, and several of the church men began folding the tables. Even though he was not a member, Jimmy Johns insisted on working right alongside his good friend, Rex.

Matt noted with interest that one small group had formed over by the bird bath and showed no signs of leaving. He wouldn't have thought much about it except for the strange mixture of people making up the group. Seated in folding chairs were Mrs. Emmaline Harris, Jimbo, and Vance Morgan (who had not even attended the picnic.) Their rapt attention was focused on an agitated Bernie Coggins who was pacing back and forth waving his arms.

"Matt, what do you think is going on?" Libbie asked as she slipped up next to him. "One minute Aunt Emma was helping me pack up, and the next thing I know, she's over there with the guys. She's been acting a little strange all weekend, too. Like last night, she went out on one of her unannounced evening walks again. I heard her slip out the kitchen door around 9:15. I waited for awhile, then really started to get worried and was about to call you when she snuck back in around 10:30.

"You know, even though things were starting to calm down around here, she just doesn't need to be going out alone like that at night. Travis would have a fit if he knew - especially now after Velma's break-in Friday night."

Matt rubbed his chin and stared at the group for a minute before answering. "I don't know, Lib, but there's no reason we shouldn't go join them is there? Come on," he said, taking her by the arm.

Elizabeth Borden Whitestone was amazed that Matt's familiar use of Lib, an old nickname which had seldom been used by anyone but Rob, was both comforting and welcome.

Chapter 32

Whatever your years, there is in every being's heart the love of wonder, the undaunted challenge of events, the unfailing childlike appetite for "What next?" and the joy of the game of life.
General Douglas MacArthur

Monday morning arrived with a mixture of excitement, anticipation, and apprehension, as it ushered in the last week of October. The children in the community were busy putting together costumes, planning for a fun, productive Halloween night on Tuesday. The parents were slightly less excited and a good bit more cautious this year, considering the events of the summer and the fact that neither the murder suspect who had been seen in their area nor the drug gang members had been apprehended. In addition, Velma's break-in over the weekend had quite a few folks on edge.

Jimbo and Shelley had managed to revive some enthusiasm with their long-awaited announcement in Sunday's paper confirming that the surprise celebrity would, indeed, be arriving on Wednesday and would be staying at the Hopkin's House Inn through the Seafood Festival weekend. No, it would not be the President. However, Malcolm Steinbeck, an award-winning Hollywood Producer would be visiting, considering their area for his next movie which would be based on a best-selling novel. The citizens of Apalachicola were pleased with the announcement and especially excited about the possibilities. The cheerleaders were slightly disappointed but determined to come up with another suitable welcoming cheer by Wednesday. In fact, Amber, one of the seniors, hinted that she was entertaining the hope of a possible part in the movie.

Everyone was making last minute plans for the festival which would officially begin at 4:00 P.M. on Friday with a pop band on stage at Battery Park overlooking the bay. The festivities were expected to attract a record 20,000 people this year due, in part, to the newest Friday night event.

As in years past, the Sea Festival King and Miss Florida Seafood would arrive together aboard the Governor Stone Schooner to usher in the opening ceremonies. But this year after the ceremony, amid a fanfare of music and fireworks, they would lead their procession to the gazebo stage at the park where the storytelling contest would begin as soon after 6:00 as possible.

The Seafood Festival had long been billed as Florida's oldest maritime and seafood spectacle. Its founding purpose had been to celebrate the smorgasbord of seafood abounding in the local waters, as well as to recognize the many mariners who harvested the world-renowned oysters, shrimp, and various fish from the sea. Thus it was no surprise that among the most popular events each year were the oyster-shucking contest where contestants were judged on their neatness as well as quickness, and the oyster-eating contest in which some of the more competitive consumers guzzled down two hundred and fifty to three hundred raw oysters during a fifteen minute span.

Also quite popular was the Saturday afternoon Blessing of the Fleet where clergymen, joined by the King of the festival and Miss Florida Seafood, blessed a river parade of fishing, shrimping, and oystering vessels as well as privately owned sailboats, cruisers and speedboats who chose to join in. And in the last few years, the weekend had expanded to include a Saturday night Ball at which the King, traditionally recognized as Retsyo, the son of Neptune, was honored and given the task of guarding and protecting the natural resources of the inland waters, bays, and estuaries throughout the coming year.

Other planned activities on Saturday included the maritime marathon which was a five- thousand meter race on Saturday morning, a downtown parade at 10:00, where the cheerleaders would perform on the high school float which followed the marching band, and a blue crab race - always a popular event with the children. The culminating activities on Sunday provided gospel music entertainment featuring spiritual singers from around the state. Throughout the weekend, the downtown and riverfront area would offer numerous art, craft, and food booths with musical groups performing on various corners and in the park.

"Little wonder I love this place so much," Sam Penton thought as he sat in his office late Monday evening proofreading the final copy of the Seafood Festival program. The program committee had spared few expenses this year, determined to add an air of professionalism to the festivities.

The ten-page booklet was well-laid out with an introduction and welcome by the mayor on the inside front cover followed by a history of the festival, table of contents, a map, various articles on events, and local advertisements on the last few pages. The inside back cover featured a page for the kids to color with pictures of various fish native to the area. Throughout the booklet were trendy pin and ink illustrations contributed by Libby and her art group. A colored picture of Governor Stone graced the glossy front cover.

The phone on Sam's desk rang, sounding obnoxiously loud in the quiet of the otherwise deserted newspaper building. "Who in the world would be calling here after 11:00 at night?" he wondered, knowing that Annie had gone to bed hours ago. Disgruntled at the intrusion, he picked up the receiver and barked, "Sam Penton here."

"Sam? Man am I glad you're there." Bernie Coggins wheezed on the other end of the line. "We got 'em, Sam! We got the big guys this time. Those feds and I, we intercepted their big load way back up in a swampy slew of Gator's Hell. You won't believe how much they were running...this was some kind of big-time operation.

"Hey, can you come on down to the station? I know it's late, but we need to get this news out as soon as possible with the festival coming and all."

By the time Sam arrived home it was after 2:00 A.M., much too late for any newspaper coverage the next day. Nevertheless, the news was out and all over town by early morning.

The pre-dawn commercial fishermen were among the first to digest the information along with their thick, black morning coffee. They were having a hard time believing that the major shipments had been coming up the river right under their noses, and in a thirty-two foot sailboat.

By 8:00, the old-timers whittling group had things all figured out - almost.

"I coulda told 'em all along that those guys was coming in by water," one of them said. "It just makes sense - after Doc Rob stumbled onto that bunch at the airstrip and got himself killed, they weren't stupid enough to keep bringing the stuff in there, no sirree. But you know now, those big groups out of South America have plenty of contacts in coastal areas like ours and they don't give up too easy. I bet it didn't take 'em no time to figure out how to sneak up there into Gator's Swamp."

"What do you guys reckon they've been doing with all that stuff after they got it off the boat?" another asked. "I heard there was over fifty pounds of marijuana and cocaine on that little sailboat, hidden in a special-made compartment under the floor; Cap'n Charlie was saying it had a street value of around half a million dollars. Seems like it'd be pretty hard to move that much stuff without arousing some suspicion."

A collective grunt indicated that the group needed to reflect on the problem a while longer, so they turned their careful attention back to the little pieces of wood in their hands. They seemed to think better when they were whittling.

At noon, Sylvia's Diner at the Docks was packed and buzzing with the news. Of course, Mildred was right in the middle of things.

"Well, this is certainly a fine time for them to decide to catch those people," she huffed, "the very day before that Hollywood Producer comes to town. I'm sure he'll be real impressed with the area. Just look out the window there - cops and drug dogs roaming the docks, and those TV cameras in here from all over the state. They'll probably hang around all weekend and just ruin everything."

"Oh, I don't think so, Mildred," Shelley interrupted. "Jimbo tells me they're pretty close to wrapping this thing up now. They think they have all of the group in custody but one, and they know who he is; it's just a matter of picking him up."

"Well, I wish they'd hurry up and get on out of here," Mildred ranted on. "Who is this other person, anyway? Is it anyone from around here? I heard that the guys on the boat were Spanish and could hardly speak a word of English. One of those agents from Miami had to translate everything for Bernie....Anyway, Shelley, how does Jimbo know all about it?"

Realizing that she had said too much, Shelley figured the best way to handle the situation was with blunt honesty. "Sorry, that's all I'm at liberty to say. But I can promise that you'll all know everything within a few days."

At 6:00 Tuesday evening, Libbie was talking with Travis on the portable phone as she headed toward the front door to greet another group of trick-or-treaters.

"Mom," Travis said, "I really hate to miss the festival, but I've got a major Engineering test Monday, and besides, this weekend's homecoming you know. By the way, did I tell you that Rachel's coming up?"

"Yes, you did Honey, several times," she smiled, "and I know you'll have fun. Of course I'm disappointed, but I certainly understand...hold on, let me get the door. The kids are out in full force tonight."

Standing at the door with his face pressed up to the screen was an adorable, freckled-face little fisherman, barefooted with rolled-up overalls, a strangely familiar-looking red paisley bandanna around his neck, a straw hat, and a fishing pole over his shoulder. His little eyes sparkled as he said, "Trick or treat ma'am...and is Mrs. Harris here?"

At first Libbie was too distracted by the man standing behind the little boy to respond. She was sure that she didn't know him, but there was something - oh dear - it was the eyes! They were suspiciously like the ones on the man that Trish had identified in the picture this summer. Even behind the glasses Libbie could tell; they were penetrating yet hesitant, piercing but gentle.

Looking back at the little boy she quickly said, "I'm not sure where Mrs. Harris is right now, dear. But here, have an apple and a box of raisins."

The child's smile faded as he turned to the man. "But Uncle Jay, she told us to come trick-or-treating here tonight."

"Mom?" Travis called over the receiver. "Who is that? Is it the little boy that Aunt Emma met this summer?"

Before Libbie could answer, Emmaline Harris shuffled into the foyer.

"Well, good evening Master Jody. I've been expecting you, and don't you look nice? I told you that bandanna of my late husband's would be just the thing to complete your outfit."

Excusing herself as she stepped in front of Libbie, Emmaline opened the screen door. "Why don't you two come in and have a cool drink before you go on to the other houses? There's a doggie in here who would love to see both of you, and besides, I don't believe that you've met my niece, Libbie."

Libbie, who had completely forgotten her manners, stared awkwardly with her mouth open as the hesitant young man and the excited little boy entered her house.

"Mom? Are you there? What's going on?" Travis' voice called from the portable phone on the foyer table where Libbie had absentmindedly laid it.

Chapter 33

Every fishing water has its secrets. It has beauty and wisdom and content. And to yield up these mysteries, it must be fished with more than hooks.

Zane Gray

On Friday morning, Malcolm Steinbeck arose promptly at 5:00 as was his usual habit. Careful not to disturb his wife, Torie, he showered and shaved quickly and crept out of their guest suite at the Hopkins House in search of coffee.

The wide-plank hardwood floors in the hall creaked under the plush oriental rug runners, and several overfed calico cats who were resting comfortably on a striped, damask Queen Anne loveseat showed little concern for the intruder. They were apparently quite used to the typical moans and groans of the old nineteenth century guest house. A third cat awaited Malcolm on the top step of the grand, wide staircase leading to the parlor. It took one look at him and swished its tail toward the carved wooden banister as if instructing him to go around.

Downstairs, a gleaming silver coffee service was set up on a mahogany sideboard, and the freshly brewed coffee had a rich chicory smell reminiscent of New Orleans. The delicate china cups reminded Malcolm of his grandmother's tea set, and he thought with amusement that he could almost hear her voice instructing him to hold the cup gently by the handle with one hand rather than cradling the warm, delicate base in both hands.

"Excuse me, but do you have any styrofoam cups?" he asked a sleepy waitress who appeared to be just coming in for the day. She was tying a white linen bodice apron over her black polyester pants outfit as she came through the kitchen door, and he noticed the plastic handle of her hairbrush sticking out of the apron pocket.

His ever-present eye for beauty and talent was rewarded when she turned her face toward him. The recently brushed dark hair was pulled back in a sleek, shiny ponytail at the nape of her neck, revealing a classic oval face with large, heavily-lined brown eyes and a full mouth. Her smooth olive complexion should have been plainly beautiful, but the dark, heavy make-up line around the chin and jaws suggested that the young lady thought otherwise - or perhaps just didn't know better.

If possible, the large eyes widened when the girl recognized Malcolm Steinbeck. She straightened her tall, thin frame and quickly brushed her hands over the apron front to smooth any wrinkles.

"Oh, good morning Mr. Steinbeck. I'm so sorry, but my mind was a thousand miles away. Did you ask for something?"

Her voice was rich with a cultured southern accent that Steinbeck found delightful. His casting mind could already imagine her playing the part of Jennifer in his up-coming movie.

"And good morning to you, young lady. I know it's too early for breakfast, but today happens to be my twenty-fifth wedding anniversary, and I would like to take my wife some coffee in bed. She would love these nice little tea set cups, I'm sure, but I'm afraid that I might break them or possibly spill the coffee trying to get it upstairs and around those cats. Some nice styrofoam cups would probably be best."

"Oh, I'm sorry about those cats, sir. I told Aunt Shelley that we ought to make them stay outside, but she insists that they are part of the authentic ambiance of the old place."

"And right she is," Malcolm agreed. "My wife happens to love cats. We have several of our own. In fact, she made the comment last night that she felt very much at home when one of them rubbed against her leg."

"Well, that's sure nice to hear, sir. Look, why don't you have a seat, and I'll be right back with your cups."

The young girl returned quickly carrying a round tray which was covered with a pink linen napkin. On the tray were two pink pottery ceramic mugs and a matching carafe of coffee. The condiments were in a little silver mesh basket next to two folded pink linen napkins. In the middle of the tray was a tall, thin vase with a single long-stemmed pink rose.

"I thought that you might want something a little nicer than styrofoam since it's your anniversary," she said with an easy smile.

"What an enchanting creature," Malcolm thought. Out loud he said, "Why thank you so much, my dear."

The first streaks of morning were painting the sky as Malcolm and Torie ventured out with their coffee and sat in the high-backed wooden rockers on the porch. Their three-room suite was on the second floor, and the French doors in their sitting room opened onto a wide, wood-railed porch which ran around three sides of the large, Williamsburg style inn.

From their perch they could observe a variety of early morning activities as the citizens of Apalachicola prepared for the big weekend.

To their left were several gift shops, two of which were already putting out displays and sale racks on the sidewalk. On the corner next to the shops, a young artist was setting up his easel and chairs to do chalk pastel portraits.

Across the street in a small triangular park, several members of a bluegrass band were backing their van up to a small, makeshift wooden stage. Another member was sitting on the edge of the stage tuning his guitar. And beyond the bridge, numerous sailboats could be seen in the bay, many already decorated with the blue, green and yellow colors of this year's festival.

Malcolm slurped his last bit of coffee, took a deep breath and let out a loud, uncharacteristic "good ol' boy" belch - a touch of southern culture that Jimbo had shared with him.

"Why Malcolm Steinbeck!" his wife giggled. "Whatever has come over you?"

"I don't know, Sugar, but it sure does feel good. I'm more relaxed than I've been in a long time. In fact, I was thinking we ought to take a picnic over to that island today and get some real Florida sand in our shoes."

Trish and her roommate, Cassie, arrived home around 1:00 to an empty house. Libbie had left instructions on the refrigerator message center for them to meet her at the studio and they would all go to Sylvia's for lunch. Aunt Emma was nowhere to be found.

The girls quickly unloaded the car and Trish took a minute to give Wes a call and let him know that they had arrived safely. He would not be able to come home for the festival due to a home game that weekend, so Trish and Cassie were planning to go to Tallahassee early Sunday morning and spend most of the day there before heading back to Auburn.

At 3:30 Matt made the final check on his list as he tested the microphone on the stage at Battery Park. He looked out over the sea of folding chairs and felt nervously like a bridegroom awaiting the magic moment. *"What an interesting thought,"* he mused. As he continued to marvel at the possibilities that the evening promised, his eyes followed a sea gull soaring toward the bay, and his thoughts slipped easily into a prayer:

"Well, Father; how about this? Isn't it amazing? Here I am, once again, in complete awe of your incredible grace and plans. You know, three years ago I was questioning everything about my life...you remember, I'm sure. My heart was really sick - almost lifeless...and now, well, it has this wonderful full feeling, almost like it could burst."

Matt felt a tug on his pants leg and looked down to see two dirty little barefooted children with cotton candy all over their sticky hands and faces.

"Mister," said the older of the two, a little boy, "Can me and my sister say something on that microphone?"

Matt knelt down next to the children. "Well, I think that can be arranged," he said. "Who wants to go first?"

"I do, I do!" they yelled simultaneously.

"OK kids, I have an idea," Matt said, glancing across the park. "See that little lady over there by the palm tree putting up signs - no, actually I believe she's taking those signs down, although I'm not sure why...." The children nodded. "Anyway, I want you both to climb up in this chair - careful now - and lean toward the microphone. When I say 'go,' both of you yell 'Vote for Mrs. Harris.' If you say it loud enough, I promise you that she'll give you some goodies out of that basket that she's carrying."

As Matt adjusted the microphone for the children, he murmured a soft "Thank you, God, and Amen."

Chapter 34

A diamond is simply a chunk of coal made good under pressure.

Source Unknown

"Good evening ladies and gentlemen, boys and girls, citizens and visitors. I am Rev. Matthew Douglas, and it has been my pleasure to chair this year's Seafood Festival. Tonight I would like to welcome you to the first of what we hope will be many 'Biggest Mouth in Town' contests.

"We have been overwhelmed with the results of the ballot sales. As of 3:00 today, the event had raised $5,258.00. Your wonderful turnout this evening will certainly raise that amount significantly, and we hope to announce a final figure and a winner before the evening is over.

"We know that you will not be disappointed. These contestants have practiced and campaigned diligently for weeks, and we just hope that you are as excited as they are.

"Before we begin, I would like to explain the rules and ask for your cooperation. Each contestant will be limited to ten minutes, and they will not be allowed to use any props other than this stool if they should choose to sit. You may clap when a contestant is introduced and when they finish, but please be respectful during their storytime and refrain from any clapping or otherwise distracting noises, excluding laughter, of course.

"The contestants have drawn numbers for the order in which they will appear, and I know that you are as anxious as they are to get started, so let's get this show on the road. It is my great pleasure to welcome our first storyteller, Mr. Jimbo Hopkins."

The crowd burst forth with applause, and a whole row of Jimbo's charter boat crew stood up, whistling and yelling "Go Jimbo, go!" Malcolm and Torie were sitting on the first row by the stage, and they gave Jimbo a big thumbs up as he sauntered up to the mike. He obviously was their choice to win as they were staying at his inn, and they had grown quite fond of Jimbo and Shelley in the last few days. In fact, upon entering the park that evening, Malcolm had made an anonymous $1,000.00 donation in Jimbo's name

Predictably, Jimbo captured the audience with his down-home story about the first bomb shelter ever built in Apalachicola. He recalled that it was built in the late sixties during the country's first wave of nuclear war paranoia.

"I was just a high school kid working construction during the summer when this rich lady from Canada built her summer home down here and insisted on one of them basement shelters. We told her that people just didn't put basements in around here - too flat and the water table too high and all, but no sir, she said she'd rather risk a little water than a nuclear fallout. So sure enough, the first week that she's in that house one of them monsoon rains comes and, yeah, you guessed it. My boss gets a call that very night. Seems the lady's basement's leaking, and "yours truly" here gets sent the next morning to see about it.

"Now picture this....

Mrs. Canada, she's got her washer and dryer down there, right? So that morning after breakfast she goes down to wash some clothes. Well, the water's drippin' in right on her head by the washer, and it's already got the floor pretty wet, so she grabs one of her son's football helmets and a pair of cleats off of the shelf and puts them on.

Now while she's down there, she decides to go ahead and wash the gown and bathrobe that she has on, so she takes them off and throws them in the washer. OK, are you with me here, folks? Sure you are, and don't you know that about that time I trot right on in the outside back door of the basement, 'cause my boss, he had told me to just go in that way and not disturb the lady so early in the morning.

People, I'm gonna tell you I've never been so shocked in my life. Here's this lady standing there in her birthday suit wearing a football helmet and some clown-size cleats, and she's screaming bloody murder! I'm here to tell you it took all I could do to keep from laughing. But my daddy taught me to respect my elders, so I knew I better get out of there fast."

Jimbo stopped a minute for the laughter to die down and scratched the new stubble of beard on his jaw. His eyes had a mischievous twinkle as he leaned toward the audience.

"Well, I tell you friends, I looked at that lady and I said, "I'll come back later, Ma'am." And I just couldn't help but add, "And Ma'am, I sure hope your team wins."

At this point, the audience was hysterical and Jimbo had to wait, once again, to finish. "Now if any of you are wondering why you never met the lady," he continued, "It's probably because she packed up that week and left town. I don't reckon she's been back since....and you know, I never did figure out what team she was on."

Jimbo took a deep bow and made his way off of the stage, waving with both hands. At the bottom of the steps Sam and Soloman were exchanging looks of concern as the applause for Jimbo seemed unending.

"Man, we've got our work cut out for us," Sam remarked. Next to them Mrs. Emmaline Harris simply smiled and said, "Give it your best shot, gentlemen. I've already got tonight sewn up."

Sam did, indeed, thrill the audience with his folk tale about Ol' Gator Joe who wrestled alligators bare-handed and skinned them for a living. About the only time Ol' Joe ever saw another human being was when Sam would venture up to take him supplies several times during the year and bring the gator skins back to sell to a traveling buyer. The audience was spell-bound and amazed that such a creature really existed, and Sam invited them to come by the newspaper office to see pictures..."Since we weren't allowed to use any props tonight." Sam received a standing ovation.

Next came Soloman, who was delightful as he took the hand microphone and sat on the edge of the stage to tell his story. He began by warning the parents of small children that his was a ghost story. "I just want you all to know ahead of time, in case anyone has a problem with it. But let me say that my grandpappy used to tell it to us grandchildren, and it didn't harm none of us a bit. In fact, if you ask me, the stuff that these kids see on television today makes this story look like Walt Disney." Not a single parent or child left.

Soloman's deep, resonant voice was mesmerizing, and even the crickets seemed to quieten under the spell that he wove. He cleverly tantalized the audience, carrying them in the final seconds to the base of the old moss-covered tree from which the moss lady had allegedly draped her scraggly gray arms around the charter boat captain's neck, and anyone else's who was foolish enough to linger there. The power of suggestion that she could still be seen on moonlit nights was strong, and Soloman noted with amusement that some people in the audience were starting to fidget and glance around, some even holding their necks as if fighting off the wiry lady.

At this point, Big Soloman stood up, and with his eyes wide, looked out beyond the crowd toward the bay. He pointed and spoke in a deep, slow voice. "Now if you all will turn around real easy-like and look over at that big oak tree behind you, you might just see her....shhh...real quiet now." His voice was mesmerizing, almost a whisper.

As if on cue, the wind whipped up off of the bay, stirring the scraggly strands of moss in the old tree. A collective murmer rose from the crowd, just before Big Soloman jumped off of the stage with the microphone in his hand and boomed "Gotcha!"

Adults, as well as children, screamed and laughed at the same time, then burst into applause. Off stage, Matt was laughing and shaking his hands which were red from clapping. *"We'll need to buy an applause meter for next year,"* he thought.

Big Soloman extended his large hand to Emmaline Harris as she started up the steps to the stage. "They're all yours, Mrs. Harris," he said. "I just got them good and warmed up for you."

"I'll say you did, Soloman. You're going to be a tough act to follow, but I think that I've got a winner tonight." The diminutive little lady hobbled slowly across the stage, and a respectful hush settled over the audience.

"And now, last but certainly not least, it is my pleasure to welcome Mrs. Emmaline Harris," Matt announced as she approached the microphone.

"Yay, yay Mrs. Harris," a small voice yelled before being drowned out by applause.

Emmaline adjusted the mike down and flashed her most beguiling smile at the crowd.

"Good evening to all of you who are privileged to be here tonight in The Oyster Capital of the World. I would like to begin with a little poem that seems not only appropriate for the location, but the occasion tonight as well."

The former Drama teacher folded her hands in front of her blue-flowered dress and struck a dignified pose before beginning her recitation.

A frustrated oyster in our midst did dwell,
unhappy because of some sand in his shell.
This flaw in his core seemed a miserable fate,
and he struck out at others with vengeance and hate.
But he found that his actions produced only strife,
and he realized that he wanted much more out of life.
So he said to the sand, "If I cannot remove you,
then I'll just get busy and try to improve you!"
Soon that grain of sand that had bothered him so
became a great pearl with a beautiful glow.
And all who beheld it proclaimed it quite grand;
they marveled that once it had been only sand!
"Dear friends," said the oyster, "you must understand,
that this was all part of God's marvelous plan."

Emmaline Harris smiled at the applause and nodded her head at the warm audience. "Thank you so much, ladies and gentlemen. And now, I would like to introduce to you my 'oyster,' and I hope that you will extend the proper courtesy and welcome to this special friend who I have invited to share the stage with me tonight." Ignoring the murmurs in the crowd, she stated firmly, "I realize that this is certainly out of the ordinary and is probably breaking some rule, but I think that the story my friend has to tell will top anything that I might have planned for tonight. I know for a fact that you will be glad to hear what he has to say.

"It will probably take him longer than the allotted ten minutes, so, again, I ask for your patience and kindness. And, of course, I officially withdraw my name from the candidacy." Holding up her hand to stifle the supportive comments from her fans, she continued, "And now, it is with tremendous pleasure and pride that I introduce to you my friend and former student, John Robert Sloane."

A gasp was heard from Trish in the second row, as the rest of the confused crowd gave a polite but hesitant welcome to the tall, blonde young man who walked across the stage. Emmaline gave him a reassuring hug and stepped over to the side of the stage where Jimbo was waiting with a chair for her. People near the stage might have seen Emmaline and Jimbo share a wink.

Jay cleared his throat and adjusted the microphone back up. "Good evening," he said with a shaky voice. "Like Mrs. Harris told you, my name is John Robert Sloane, but my friends call me Jay - that is the few friends I've got. You see, well, I ain't had too many friends lately 'cause I've pretty much been staying away from people. So, that might explain why I'm real uncomfortable up here in front of y'all." He stopped and looked over at Mrs. Harris with a look of desperation as he wiped his forehead. She smiled calmly, nodded her head, and softly called, "Go on son, you can do this."

Jay took a deep breath and continued. "Well, I'm mostly here tonight to try to explain some things to everyone and to apologize for some things too. And I'm hoping you'll try to understand and maybe give me a chance to start over again.

"I guess I ought to start by telling you something about myself. I pretty much grew up in Panama City, and I was in Mrs. Harris' English class in the eleventh grade. I was living with my ma at the time and things were pretty bad. My old man had moved out of town a few years earlier, but he would come around every once in a while and get pretty rough with Mom and me. He was a right big man and Ma was pretty scrawny; neither of us put up much of a fight. Mrs. Harris was the only person in my life right then that made me feel like I was worth anything. She used to tell me that God loved me, and so did she.

"Anyway, one day my old man went too far, and I just took off. I quit school, took $100.00 out of Ma's cookie jar and ran. The next thing I knew, the cops were looking for me in connection with my own mom's death. Hey, I figured that my old man did it, but I knew no one would ever believe me - especially since nobody really much knew that he came around. So, I just kept on running. I was hurtin' real bad about my mom and all, and I was so angry at my old man, and there wasn't nothing I could do about it.

"Now you kids here tonight, I hope you listen real good and learn some things. The main thing is don't ever let anybody treat you bad. If someone hurts you, tell a grown-up that you can trust. If I had talked with Mrs. Harris back then, I wouldn't have made the mistakes you're hearing about tonight." Jay stopped again and cleared his throat with a nervous cough.

"So anyway, when my money ran out, I ended up here in Apalachicola. I was scared to try to get a job because somebody might recognize me, so I slept around in old abandoned buildings and trailers. Believe me, kids, you don't ever want to do that; spiders and snakes ain't good roommates.

"Well, one morning, I snuck into the back of a newspaper delivery truck and hitched a ride out to the island. I had been peeping in windows around town just looking for easy stuff to steal, but It didn't take me long to realize that the island was the place to be. A lot of houses out there stayed vacant most of the time, and most of them had pantries full of canned goods.

"Pretty soon I wasn't just taking food, but I was stealing money and valuable stuff that I could sell, too. I even broke into a few cars, but that got too risky, especially when I hit one of the drug dealer's cars. Man, they ain't too forgiving. Anyway, my thievin' is how I got mixed up with the drug dudes. I found out real fast that they were the only ones crooked enough to buy my stolen goods.

"Well, things went from bad to worse, and by this summer, I was into stuff that was really making me uncomfortable. I was running scared all the time, and my anger was just about out of control - more like my old man than I wanted to be. And this is where the story changes, folks.

"A very special person named Bubbles stumbled into my life one night, and she made me go to a tent revival meeting. Now I've still got a lot to learn, but I am here to tell y'all that the man upstairs let me know that night that He had been watching over me all along, just waiting until I was at the end of my rope, so He could pull me back.

"So I started going to those meetings, and about the same time I finally got in touch with Mrs. Harris, and from then on my life has been turning around. Mrs. Harris, she loved me and believed in me even after I told her everything." Jay smiled rather mischievously and added, "She even snuck out of her house a few times at night to meet with me and help me decide what to do. Anyway, she convinced me to go to Sheriff Coggins, and after I confessed everything to him, he came up with a good suggestion.

"Me and him met with some drug and narcotic agents from Miami, and they worked out a kind of swap thing with me. The deal was if I would work with them and help bust the drug operation, and if I also paid back the people I had robbed plus put in one hundred hours of community service work, they would make sure that I got immunity from prosecution. By the way, they told me that the murder charge against me had been dropped last month when my old man was picked up in Tennessee and he confessed to killing my mom.

"Some of the conditions of the immunity deal weren't too hard, because more than half of what I had stolen was still stored in an old tank out on Highway 98. But I am still working to pay off the rest of it...and now I guess you're wondering how and where I've been working.

"Well, Mrs. Harris and the sheriff asked Mr. Jimbo Hopkins if I could help him at the docks. They explained everything to him, and he was real nice about it. So I changed my looks - sort of went undercover. I had already lost a bunch more weight from running all the time, messing with drugs, and not eating right. So I cut and died my hair and got these glasses, and no one recognized me from that picture that was in the paper this summer...well, almost no one, but that's a different story for another night, folks." He winked at Beverly before continuing.

"Now Mr. Jimbo's been paying me half of my wages and putting the other half in a special fund so I can pay taxes out of it and be paying you good folks back what I owe. It's probably going to take me a long time, but for the first time in my life, I know that I'm finally doing something right." Jay stopped again, taking off his glasses and cleaning them on his T-shirt.

"Okay, so I guess you all know by now about them catching those drug guys. But what you don't know is how it all happened. The sheriff and Mrs. Harris thought you might like to know the whole story, and that's the other reason I'm here tonight; they asked me to tell you about it as part of my community service. So, here goes....

"Well, about four years ago this big drug cartel out of Colombia began shipping drugs into Port St. Joe. They had a contact over there who ran the bingo parlor which was really just a front for their operation. All of the stuff was re-packaged in this guy's building after it came in from South America, and then it was trucked out around the southeast.

"Do you people remember that body that washed up after the tornado last year? OK, well his name was Edward Parker, and he was Mr. Vince Morgan's half-brother. He had been working at the bingo parlor in St. Joe until he got wise to their operation and threatened to turn them in. And not long after he discovered what was going on, he mentioned it one night to his brother on the phone. He had no idea that Mr. Morgan worked undercover for the F.B.I. Anyway, the very next week Parker came up missing.

"Y'all might have figured out by now that's why Mr. Morgan and his family moved here last year. He was hoping he'd find his brother, but he was also real committed to working with the government to catch those drug dudes. His nephew, Rex Parker- Mr. Edward Parker's son, had just gotten out of the navy, and he moved here this summer to try to help his uncle. Some of you probably know him; he works over at Riverside Congregational Church.

"Anyway, back to the drug group. They just moved their operation a little farther east after they closed up the bingo parlor, and they started using that old abandoned airfield between St. Joe and here. That's where Mrs. Harris' niece's husband, Dr. Whitestone, ran across them and got himself killed that morning when he was out hunting."

Throughout his speech, Jay had successfully avoided looking over to his right where earlier he had seen Mrs. Libby Borden's daughter, Trish, sitting. Now he dared to cast a quick glimpse in her direction, and his knees almost buckled. The petite blonde was staring at him with a hollow expression, tears rolling down her face.

"Man, maybe this is one of those times I ought to pray to You, God," he thought, and knew then that he just had.

Jay cast a look of anguish at Mrs. Harris, who was completely aware of the situation. She simply crossed her arms and gave him a reassuring smile. Jay looked back out at the crowd and felt the mystifying strength to continue.

"Now you folks already know that these drug dudes are pretty clever, so it didn't take them long to find a real good front man and runner right here in Apalachicola. And this guy helped them find a new way to bring the stuff in. They just came right up the bay out of the gulf and into the river on up into the back swamps. Nobody paid them any attention 'cause they looked like all the other folks who sail around in those family-like sailboats. And their new contact had a stoolie who would meet them way back up there in the slew. His name is Scotty and he drives a little gray, shortbed pick-up truck with a camper shell on the back.

"So anyway, these dudes would load all of the drugs in Scotty's truck and then head south. Scotty, he would bring all of the stuff to the contact man, Mr. Billy Jernigan, who would pack it in smaller, individual beauty supply boxes from his wife's shop and deliver it around the state in his eighteen-wheeler."

Several gasps, presumably from Velma's customers gave Jay time to catch his breath.

"Now don't go jumpin' to conclusions here, ladies; Mrs. Velma didn't know nothing about this. Mr. Billy and those guys had a pretty smart code system set up. When it was getting close to a delivery time, the drug dudes would send Mr. Billy fake travel brochures about cruises. The numbers in the return address would always be the date and time of the delivery, so Mr. Billy would be expectin' them. Then he would start collecting empty boxes from the shop, and he'd put them out back for Scotty to pick up at night. When he had boxes for Scotty, he would turn one of Mrs. Velma's pink flamingoes halfway around as a signal. The night before a shipment was due, he would turn the flamingo all the way around backwards.

"Well, Scotty started running a little scared after the cops questioned him a few times- once for suspicion of drugs when they searched his house but didn't find nothing, and another time when they questioned him on a hit and run. His truck was seen speeding near Mrs. Harris' house the morning their little dog got hit." Jay once again glanced nervously over at Trish who was now smiling slightly and nodding her head.

"So anyway, Scotty decided to take matters into his own hands and go inside Mrs. Velma's shop from then on to get the boxes. He couldn't get keys from Mr. Billy because he was out of town, so he just stole some keys to the shop from Bubble's sister, Beverly, who was working there. The two of them had been going out some. Well, when she found out, he threatened her pretty bad to keep her quiet. It scared her so much that she quit her job at Velma's and has pretty much been laying low since then.

"Now if you're wonderin' how I've been involved in all of this, I'm about to tell you, and I'm not proud of any of it but the last part. See, I met Scotty one night at a lounge out on 98, and he started me messing around with drugs. And you kids, listen to me real good here. Scotty, he pretended to be my buddy and all, and since I didn't have any friends around here, that was fine with me. Well, at first he would just give me a smoke or two. Pretty soon, he said I needed to pay him because he was sort of down on his luck. Then he started trying to sell me stronger, more expensive stuff, especially when he found out that I had all of that jewelry and stolen money. No, he wasn't my friend, kids. In fact, he ended up nearly killing me one night after he stole everything I had on me. That's when I woke up and, with the help of Bubbles and the good Lord, realized that there had to be more to life than what I was seeing. So, I decided to take some action, and went to see Mrs. Harris and then the sheriff.

"With Sheriff Coggins' knowledge, I started doing a little undercover work so to speak. Beverly had told me about Scotty and the keys, so I knew something must be going on at the beauty parlor. In fact, that's where I met Rex by accident one night, and when we realized that we were after the same dudes, we started working together- which was a good thing, because Scotty didn't much trust me anymore after he had treated me so bad.

"We got with the feds who helped us arrange for Rex to meet up with Scotty, posing as a rich dude looking to buy a big stash. Scotty told Rex that he'd have a big supply the following week when the next shipment came in. So we started taking turns watching Velma's every night, not sure what we were looking for, but knowing there had to be some connection."

Jay now had the audience in the palm of his hand, and he stopped again to clear his throat. Out of the crowd, a little boy came running up and climbed onto the stage with a can of cola in his hand.

"Here Uncle Jay; Mom says your voice must be awful tired by now. Can I stay up here with you, Uncle Jay - please?" Jody reached out and took Jay's hand. "I'll help ya' if you need me to," he beamed. Jay felt a tug on his heart as Jody looked at him with a look of pure adoration.

"Sure you can, Little Buddy."

Turning back to the audience, Jay said, "Folks, with the help of one of my best new friends here, I'm going to wrap this thing up. Now, let's see; where was I? Oh yeah, last Friday night; well, we about hit pay dirt. When Scotty showed up at Velma's, me and Rex hid in the bushes out back, and then Rex jumped in the back of the camper when Scotty pulled off. Rex had his cellular phone with him, and he was talking with me and the sheriff and the feds the whole time he was riding. But ol' Scotty just went home that night and nothing happened. So me and Rex hung out near his house all day Saturday waiting.

"Do you folks remember that bad weather that came through last Saturday night? Well, the drug dudes had planned to come in that night, but the weather was so bad that they had to delay their run. But, sure enough, Monday night Scotty jumped in that truck around 9:00 and took off. We had seen him go out earlier and put something in the truck, so Rex was waiting to jump in the back if he needed to. I've gotta tell you folks, that was pretty brave in my book. Anyway, the minute they took off, Rex called us on his phone from the camper shell of the truck and we followed not too far behind them. Shoot, if Rex hadn't given us such good descriptions of where they were going, we would have lost them, because we couldn't get too close on those dark roads out of town. And we would have never found that place way up in Gator's Hell.

"Now, most of you probably don't know Rex, but if y'all don't mind, I'd like for him to come on up here now so you can meet him."

"Yeah, let's hear it for Rex," Matt yelled, surprising even himself. The crowd answered with cheers and applause. A shy, red-faced Rex stood up and waved, then tried to sit back down, until Beverly gave him a push toward the stage. Jay and Jody walked over to the steps and pulled him up on the stage and back toward the microphone.

"Now the way I see it, folks, Rex here is your real hero, and I'm just a plain old guy who's done some bad stuff and is trying to make up for it."

"No you're not a bad guy, Uncle Jay," Jody whined, and wrapped his little arms around Jay's waist.

"He's certainly not," Mrs. Harris chimed in as she walked across the stage.

"Hey now, let's hear it for these guys," Jimbo called out as he joined the group.

The crowd was on their feet, louder than they had been all night. Several of the cheerleaders near the stage started a cheer and people around them joined in......

"Hip-hip hooray, for Rex and Jay!"

From the back of the crowd, a short, stout little girl/lady made her way toward the stage. An older gentleman was following her, and she kept shooing him back. When she reached the steps, she reached for Matt's hand and he helped her climb carefully, slowly, two feet per step. Upon reaching the stage, she smiled and waved at the lively audience whose applause grew even louder. She giggled and waved some more before going over to Emmaline Harris and giving her a big hug. As the crowd began to calm down, she made her way over to Jay and Rex at the microphone, and flashing her large brown, doe-like eyes along with a saucy little grin said, "Hello; I'm Bambi and you guys are my new 'hewos.' I've been looking for a husband. Tell me; are you married?" The crowd erupted once more.

Libbie had joined Matt down by the steps and, caught up in the spirit of the moment, she enthusiastically grabbed his hand and squeezed it.

"Matt, this has been the most wonderful festival opening that I can remember! You're a pretty special guy - do you know that?"

Matt removed his hand from hers and casually put his arm around her shoulder. "Yeah, pretty lady, but I try to keep it a secret."

Libbie leaned into his broad shoulders as if it was the most natural thing in the world. "By the way, Matt," she said, "what time does the service start at your church on Sunday?"

On the front row just a few yards away from Matt and Libbie, Malcolm Steinbeck turned to his wife, Torie. "Honey, how would you like to stay around here a little longer than we had planned?"

Epilogue

Friday, December 1, continued

The Governor Stone was slowly turning in the direction of the riverfront docks. Once again, Jay adjusted his damp, fuzzy beard and practiced his deepest "Ho, ho ho."

When the Christmas committee had bestowed on him the honor of being Santa Claus this year, they had explained that he could count it towards his community service hours. Jay had been quite flattered and, most of all, touched that the village citizens would allow him the privilege of portraying the kind, benevolent old gentleman who represented the opposite of everything that Jay had ever been. He had even considered turning the offer down, but Mrs. Harris had very quickly let him know that he was not only the unanimous choice, but that he was also very worthy and deserving. "God hasn't finished with you yet, son," she had assured him. "So just settle back and enjoy the ride."

Her words rang true in his ears now, as he admitted to himself that the present ride - not only in his life, but tonight on the old schooner - was, indeed, getting better by the minute.

Letting go of the anchor rope, he clasped his hands together in prayer-like fashion and, looking toward the sky, offered a quick thanks for his new friends and home. A little boy on shore could be heard yelling, "See Mommy - here comes Santa Claus.... and look, Mommy, he's saying his prayers! Do you think he knows God?"